CRUELTY free SHOPPER

LIS HOWLETT

BLOO

First published 1989

Text copyright © 1989 Lis Howlett

Illustrations copyright © 1989 Juliet Breese

Bloomsbury Publishing Limited, 2 Soho Square,
London W1V 5DE

British Library Cataloguing in Publication Data

A CIP catalogue record for this book is available
from the British Library

ISBN 0 7475 0467 9

10 9 8 7 6 5 4 3 2 1

Printed in Great Britain by
Richard Clay Ltd, Bungay, Suffolk

contents

Welcome to this new edition of *The Cruelty-Free Shopper* — a practical guide for those who have made the decision to end, or at least join the swing towards ending, their dependence on animal products, whether for food, clothing or any other commodity. The *Shopper* is also designed as a stimulus for those who are still considering this step, perhaps daunted by the 'lack of choice' frequently associated with the adoption of such a lifestyle. Whichever category they fall into, readers will find in the following pages literally thousands of entries, organized into clear, easy-to-consult sections, along with an assortment of background and supplementary information.

The work of compilation has been carried out in close collaboration with the Vegan Society, an educational charity with a record and authority that are unrivalled in the cruelty-free field. Of all long-standing pro-animal groupings it alone can claim to have consistently promoted this supremely challenging ethic from its inception. Indeed the birth of the cruelty-free movement can rightfully be said to date from the Society's foundation in November 1944.

The vegan connection is a crucial one, since vegans have long since grasped what still eludes many: that, in the commercial sector at least, only by eliminating *all* animal involvement can you eliminate *all* animal cruelty. Properly applied, cruelty-free therefore means free of all animal ingredients and all animal testing *(see **cruelty-free criteria** on pages 143–144)*; *The Cruelty-Free Shopper* is inspired by and based on respect for this clear principle.

When using the guide please bear in mind the following:

• An asterisk (*) immediately after a company name indicates that its products are available by mail order *(see **mail-order addresses** on pages 149–150)*.
• Great care has been taken to ensure that the information provided is reliable, but since manufacturers reserve the right to make changes in the constituents, derivation and testing of their products without prior notice it should not be regarded as infallible. The *Shopper* can never be anything more than a *guide*, so make a habit of checking the ingredients listing on a product before you buy.
• The inclusion of a product should not be interpreted as an endorsement either of the product itself or of its manufactur-

introduction

er/distributor, who may pursue other commercial interests inconsistent with cruelty-free principles.

• A product's absence from these pages does not necessarily mean that it is not cruelty-free. It may have been excluded on the ground of sheer obviousness (e.g. teas, rice, tinned vegetables) or reliable information concerning its status simply may not have been available, in some cases even after quite exhaustive enquiries.

• Despite recent advances in the sphere of labelling, any one of a whole host of factors — not least the complexities of modern food science and production technology — can, at times, frustrate efforts to establish whether or not a product is entirely free of animal involvement. Moreover, the experience of compiling the *Shopper* has underlined the inescapable fact that in the final analysis even those passionately committed to the cruelty-free ethic can go only so far, and no further. To take just one ethical constraint, modern arable farming relies heavily on agrochemicals, all of which are tested — to the death — on laboratory animals; and even chemical-free organic growing supports the exploitation of animals in making use of dried blood, bone meal, hoof & horn meal and the like. The honest, if sometimes painful, acceptance of such constraints enables us to function effectively and to exert positive influence in the real, and far from ideal, world.

acknowledgements

The usefulness of this work has been increased appreciably thanks to the assistance of valued consultants, notably former Vegan Society General Secretary, Barry Kew — who researched and supplied the data which formed the basis of the introductions to the main sections, as well as the material in **alcoholic beverages** — and Drs Chris and Gill Langley, who assisted in the preparation of the **note on additives** and the **cruelty-free criteria**.

Once the blinkers of conditioning and complacency are off, the reality of farm animals' existence becomes disconcertingly clear. That reality typically comprises filthy, dimly-lit sheds; terrifying transport by lorry; market abuse; and the horror of the slaughterhouse, where 4,000 animals die *every minute of every working day* in the UK alone. This industry's business is misery, suffering, death and sheer waste — and its unnecessary products are obtained at a hidden cost far higher than any price tag can describe.

Milk is taken two to three times daily from cows made continually pregnant by artificial insemination and separated almost immediately from their calves — the rightful udder sucklers — who go to market, slaughter, fattening pen or veal crate. After 4–5 calves have been snatched from her the clapped-out cow will end up in a burger or soup tin, having lived barely a quarter of her natural lifespan.

Some 90% of British eggs are taken from debeaked hens kept 4 or 5 to a 20" x 18" cage, worn out after 1 or 2 years and slaughtered for soups, pastes, stock cubes and baby foods. Even free-range systems cannot obviate the industry's 'need' to cull 'bad layers' and suffocate 40 million day-old male chicks a year because they won't lay at all.

Cattle, pigs, sheep and poultry are routinely mutilated — castrated, dehorned, debeaked, tail-docked, ear-tagged, teeth-ground — and/or reared in appalling conditions to reach slaughter weight as quickly as possible. Over 400,000 sows spend most of their tragic lives confined individually in narrow stalls on concrete without bedding. The 450 million broiler chickens slaughtered annually in the UK are reared in tens of thousands in windowless sheds artificially dimly lit for 23.5 hours out of 24 and killed when 6–7 weeks old. These chicks are reduced to drugged, lumbering, gasping, overweight cripples. Spring chicken are slaughtered still younger, at just 26–30 days old.

Fish are mercilessly and relentlessly snatched from their natural environment, heaped up and left to die a lingering death. And, as with any animal product, their mass slaughter (60 million tonnes per annum worldwide) cannot be seen in isolation; behind the fish in the freezer is not only their horror story but also the deliberate or incidental death of tens of thousands of seals, dolphins and porpoises.

In the light of the above, for how much longer can so many of us to close our eyes to the fact that the systematic exploitation of non-human animals for their bodies and products causes more avoidable suffering than any other force on earth?

To conclude on a more practical note, the cruelty-free shopper should be aware that animal derivatives in food are not always as glaringly obvious as a chunk of meat or a slab of fish. Insidious ingredients to watch out for include gelatine (especially in desserts and confectionery); lactose (a milk sugar used extensively as a carrier for flavouring agents, especially in savoury snacks such as crisps); vitamin D_3 (derived from either lanolin or fish oil); so-called 'vegetable margarines' which contain whey powder; misleading names — like 'oleo oil' for beef fat; and such "who'd have thought it?" items as anchovies in Worcester sauce. For those venturing beyond the boundaries of this guide steering clear of the 'nasties' generally requires no more effort than a quick read of the label.

recommended reading

Assault and Battery, Mark Gold, Pluto Press, 1983

baked goods

Bread: 100% Stoneground Wholemeal, 100% Stoneground Wholemeal Cob, 100% Wholemeal, Soft Wholemeal; *Rolls:* Wholemeal Dinner, Wholemeal Snack; 100% Stoneground Wholemeal Baps, Wholemeal Fruited Teacakes, Wholemeal Fruit Loaf, Wholemeal Malt Loaf, Wholemeal Muffins

ALLINSON

Wrapped Bread: Brown Sliced, Stoneground Wholemeal Sliced, White Sliced, Wholemeal Sliced; Bran Crumpets, Crumpets, Hovis Mini Loaves, Muffins, Pitta Bread, Potato Cakes, Teacakes, White Baps, Wholemeal Baps, Wholemeal Muffins, Wholemeal Pitta Bread

ASDA

Country Grains: Sliced, Unsliced; Country Loaf/Rolls; Extra-Fibre White Loaf/Rolls; Shapers Loaf/Rolls; Sliced Wholemeal Bread, Wholemeal Rolls

BOOTS

Uncut Crusty Bread: Bloomer White, Coburg White, Farmhouse White, Split Tin White, Tin White

BRITISH BAKERIES

Large Bread: 100% Organic Wholemeal, 100% Wholemeal, Granary; *Small Bread:* 100% Wholemeal, Fruit Bread, Granary Tin, Sunflower Seed; *Rolls:* 100% Wholemeal, Granary; Pitta Bread

CERES

White Soft Grain: Extra Thick, Medium, Thick

CHAMPION

Brown Bread: Medium-Sliced; *White Bread:* Medium-Sliced, Square Sliced, Thick-Sliced, Thin-Sliced; *Wholemeal Bread:* Goodlife Medium-Sliced, Goodlife Thi-

CO-OP

ck-Sliced; *Baps:* Soft White, Goodlife Wholemeal; Crumpets, Fruited Teacakes, Soft White Finger Rolls

CRUSTY GOLD   Bloomer, Farmhouse, French Stick, Split Tin

FARMSTEAD   *Country Baps:* White, Brown

FINE LADY   *Loaves:* Oaten, Stoneground, White Sliced, Wholemeal; *(wholemeal)* Granary Cobs, Oaten Rolls; Finger Rolls, Sesame Burger Buns, Vienna Cob Rolls

GOSWELL BAKERIES   *Rolls:* Bagels, Plain Oven, Platzels; *Speciality Breads:* Black Rye, Light Rye, Polish Rye, Seedless Rye; *Stoneground Wholemeal:* Cerea Traditional, Continental-Style, Daktyla, Fruit Sesame, Granary; Daktyla *(white)*

HOVIS   *Sliced:* Country Grain, Family Wheat Germ, Golden Bran, Handy Hovis, Stoneground Wholemeal; *Rolls & Baps:* Country Grain Rolls, Stoneground Baps, Stoneground Mini-Loaves; *Sliced Granary:* Malted Brown, Malted Wholemeal

INTERNATIONAL HARVEST   *Pitta Breads:* Mini-White, White, Wholemeal

JUVELA   Low-Protein Loaf

KEMPENAAR   *Part-baked:* Burger Buns, French Stick White, French Stick Wholemeal, Poppy Seed Rolls, White Party Rolls, White Rolls, Wholemeal Party Rolls

KOLOS BAKERY   *Bread:* 100% Rye, Bauernbrot (German Rye), Bavarian 100% Rye, Canadian Wholewheat, Crusty, Estonian, French Sticks, Italian, Large Brown, Large Round White, Large White, Organic Wholewheat,

Small Granary, Small Rye, Small White *(sliced and unsliced)*, Ukrainian Rye, Vienna; *Pitta Bread:* Brown, White

Brown Bread, White Bread **LITTLEWOODS**

Brown Bread: Drie Corn German-Style, Hi-Bran Loaf, Multi-Grain Bread, Nutty Cob, Wholemeal Picnic Mini-Pittas, Wholemeal Sandwich Bread; *Crusty Bread:* Ciabatta, Crusty, Crusty Rye German-Style, French Baton/Cob/Petit Pain, French Crusty Bread & Rolls, Stoneground Wholemeal Farmhouse; *Fruited & Fancy:* Malt Loaf, Wholemeal Hot-Cross Buns; *Hot-Plate Items:* Crumpets, Pikelets, Plain Muffins, Potato Farls, Raisin & Bran Muffins; *Rolls:* Bagels, Breakfast/Morning, Crusty Brown, Oatmeal, Stoneground; *Ready-to-Bake Items:* Rolls/Baguettes *(brown and white)*; *White Bread:* Batched White Loaf, Picnic Mini-Pittas, Segale Scuro **MARKS & SPENCER**

Mighty White Bread, Mighty Bites, Mighty Munchers, Mighty Muffins **MIGHTY WHITE**

Big T White Extra Thick, Danish, Danish Toaster, Premium, Traditional, White Sliced, White Uncut; *Rolls & Baps:* Burger Buns, Champion Soft Grain Baps, Crusty Ploughman's Rolls, French Stick, Long Rolls, Salad Baps, Sandwich Baps, Scotch Rolls – White; *Buns:* Chelsea Buns, Currant Buns, Fruited Teacakes, Northumbrian Teacakes; Crumpets, Muffins, Pikelets, Potato Cakes **MOTHER'S PRIDE**

Manna Loaf: Carrot & Raisin, Fruit, Sunseed **NATURAL WAY**

Square Sliced: Soft Grain, Soft Wholemeal, White **NIMBLE**

food products

OLYMPUS *Pittas:* White, Wholemeal

PEMA *(all long-life)* Graham Bread, Linseed Bread, Rice Bread, Special Bread, Wheatgerm Bread; Pumpernickel, Vollkornbrot

PREWETT'S Stoneground Wholemeal Breads

RITE-DIET Low-Protein White Bread

SAFEWAY *White Sliced:* Medium, Thick, Thin; *Soft Grain White:* Medium, Thick; *100% Wholemeal:* Medium, Thick; Bran Bread, Brown Bread Medium-Sliced, Danish Toaster *(white)*, Wheatgerm Bread, Wholemeal Tin; *Baps:* Burger, Bran, Sliced Wholemeal, Stoneground Wholemeal, White, Wholemeal; *Rolls:* Stoneground Wholemeal, White Finger, White Soft Snack, Wholemeal Finger, Wholemeal Morning; *Muffins:* White, Wholemeal; *Pitta Breads:* White, Wholemeal; *Buns:* Burger, Currant, Spiced Fruit, White Hot Cross, Wholemeal Hot Cross; Crumpets, Fruit Teacake, Potato Scones, Ready-to-Bake Mini-Baguettes

SAINSBURY *Buns:* Hot Cross, Mini Hot Cross, Mini Wholemeal Hot Cross, Spiced Fruit, Tea, Wholemeal Hot Cross; Crumpets, Pikelets, Soft-Batch Fruited Bun Loaf

SNOWCREST Pitta Bread *(frozen)*

SUNBLEST *Breads:* Danish Toaster, Danish White, Long Loaf – Brown, Long Loaf – White, White; *Baps:* Brown Salad, Farmhouse, White Salad; *Rolls:* Crusty Cob, Finger, Soft Brown; *Buns:* Currant, Spiced Fruit; Crumpets, Fruited Teacakes, Pikelets, Sunmalt Loaf, White Muffin

Loaves (organic): 100% Rye, 100% Wheat, Gluten-Free, Malt Loaf

SUNNYVALE

Loaves: Bran Loaf, Brown Breads, Crusty Bread *(all types)*, Fruit Batch, Hovis, Malt Loaf, Natural White, Soft White Batch, Stoneground Wholemeal, Stoneground Wholemeal Batch, Wheatgerm, White, Wholemeal; *Rolls:* Brown Morning, Brown Snack Wheaten, White Crusty, White High-Fibre, White Morning, White Snack; *Buns:* Fruit, Seeded Burger, Teacakes, Wholemeal Hot Cross, Wholemeal Spiced; *Baps:* Bran, Stoneground Wholemeal; *Muffins:* Scottish Muffins, Stoneground Wholemeal Muffins, Wholemeal Muffins; White Pitta Bread, Wholemeal Pitta Bread

TESCO

Bread: Harvester, HiBran, Wheatgerm; Hi-Bran Rolls

VITBE

Loaves: Brown, Brown Granary, German Rye, Italian Dark Rye, Long Thick-Sliced, Medium-Sliced Wholemeal, Oatmeal, Soft Brown with Malted Grains, Soft Grain White, Soft White, Stoneground Wholemeal Medium-Sliced, Thick-Sliced Wholemeal, Traditional White, White Crusty, White Medium-Sliced, White Sliced, Wholemeal with Oats; *Rolls:* Brown, Breakfast, Rye & Onion, White Finger, White Soft, White with Soft Grains, Wholemeal; *Buns:* Burger with Sesame Seeds, Chelsea, Hot Cross, Spiced Fruit, Wholemeal Hot Cross; *Muffins:* Brown with Malted Wheatgrains, White, Wholemeal; Crumpets, Granary Baton, Rustic Bread, Wholemeal Baps, Wholemeal French Stick, Wholemeal Sticks; *Ready-to-bake range:* Baguettes, White French-Style Bread/Rolls, Wholemeal/Granary Bread/Rolls

WAITROSE

WHOLE EARTH Stoneground Wholemeal Bread

WINDMILL BAKERY Country Brown Sliced, Hi-Fibre Wholemeal Sliced, High-Fibre White Sliced, Wholemeal Sliced, Wholemeal Thick-Sliced; Wholemeal Baps, Wholemeal Scotch Rolls

biscuits

AGLUTELLA Low-Protein Gluten-Free Cream-Filled Wafers

ASDA Bourbon Cream, Fruit Shortcake, Ginger Nut, Morning Coffee, Nice, Peanut Crunch, Rich Tea, Rich Tea Fingers

BOOTS Custard Creams, Digestive, Digestive Cream, Ginger Finger, Nice

BRAYCOT Carob Half-Coated Oatflake & Wholemeal, Mountain Cookies, Sesame Oat Crunchies

BRONTE Farmhouse Crunch, Golden Crunch, Stem Ginger

BURTON'S Rich Tea; *Snapjacks:* Country, Fruit

CO-OP Coconut Crumble Creams, Coconut Crunch, Coffee & Walnut Creams, Digestive Wheatmeal, Fig Roll, Fruit Shortcake, Ginger Nut, Lincoln, Morning Coffee, Rich Tea, Royal Duchess, Shortcake, Tangy Orange Creams

CRAWFORD'S Pennywise Wafers

DOVE'S FARM- Bourbons, Ginger Nuts *(sugar-free)*

DP *Low-Protein Chip Cookies:* Butterscotch Flavoured, Chocolate Flavoured

Coconut Drops, Cottage Crunch, Country Spice, Currant & Plain Shrewsbury, Farmhouse Oat, Flip, Lemon Drops, Mild Gingers, Priory Crumble, Shortbread, Shortbread Rings, Wholemeal, Wholewheat Ginger	**FARMHOUSE BISCUITS**
Finger Ginger, Ginger Snaps, Original Thick Tea	**FOX'S**
Gluten-Free Cookies: Coconut, Fibre, Ginger	**GF DIETARY**
Wholemeal Shortbread	**GREEN CITY**
Fruit & Nut Biscuits	**INFINITY**
Granny Ann range: High-Fibre – Original, High-Fibre – Date Syrup, High-Oat; Premier Protein Biscuit Cake	**ITONA**
Fig Rolls	**JACOBS**
Gluten-Free Low-Protein Cookies: Chocolate Chip, Cinnamon, Orange	**JUVELA**
Ginger Nuts, Ginger Thins, Tangy Orange Creams	**LITTLEWOOD'S**
Bourbon Creams, Digestive Sweetmeal, Ginger Snaps, Oat Crunchies, Plain Chocolate Biscuit Thins, Plain Chocolate Oat Crunchies, Rich Tea Fingers	**MARKS & SPENCER**
Fruit & Nut Crunch, Jaspers, Muesli Biscuits, Wholemeal Biscuits	**McVITIES**
Calbourne Crunchies range: Coconut, Ginger Parkin, Malt & Bran, Walnut	**MILLER'S DAMSEL**
Healthy Life range: Carob Chip, Ginger & Orange Cookies; Carob Mint Cookies, Carob Tropical Cookies, Muesli Cookies	**MITCHELHILL**

MOLEN AARTJE Malt Biscuits *(organic)*

NISA Bourbon Creams, Fruit Shortcake, Ginger Nuts, Round Rich Tea

OSEM Animal Biscuits, Avdat Choc Chips, Marie, Pazit, Petit Beurre; *Patisserie Cookie range:* Butter Flavour, Gadish, Madanit, Margalit; Cremugit Cookies

PEAK FREAN Shortcake

RAKUSEN Bourbon Creams, Choc Chip Cookies, Chocolate Shortcake, Custard Creams, Digestive Biscuits, Ginger Finger, Golden Crunch, Nice, Orange Creams, Shortcake Biscuits, Viennese Finger

RITE-DIET *(all gluten-free)* Bourbon Biscuits, Chocolate Chip Cookies, Custard Creams, Digestives, Lincoln – Sweet Biscuits, Muesli Cookies, Savoury Biscuits, Shortcake – Sweet Biscuits, Sweet Biscuits, Tea Biscuits; Low-Protein Chocolate-Flavour Cream Biscuits, Low-Protein Sweet Biscuits; *Low-Protein Wafers:* Chocolate, Orange, Vanilla

SAFEWAY Bourbon Creams, Digestive Sweetmeal, Fruit Shortcake, Ginger Nuts, Morning Coffee, Orange Finger Creams, Rich Tea, Rich Tea Fingers, Vanilla Wafers

SAINSBURY Apple Creams, Bourbon, Carob-Coated Ginger & Orange Fingers, Choc Chip Oat & Coconut Crunch, Chocolate Chip Nibble Cookies, Coconut Crumble Creams, Coffee & Walnut Creams, Digestive Sweetmeal, Fruit Rustics, Fruit Shortcake, Ginger Snaps, Morning Coffee, Oat and Chocolate Cookies, Peanut Crunch, Plain Chocolate Digestive Biscuits, Plain Chocolate Ginger Biscuits, Plain Chocolate

Orange Biscuits, Plain Chocolate Rustics, Rich Tea, Rich Tea Finger, Rustics

Husky Bran Biscuits **SCOTT'S**

Slymbran Digestives **SLYMBRAND**

Raspberry Wafers; *Chocolate Fingers:* Mint, Plain; *Wafer Biscuits:* Chocolate, Lemon, Orange **SNOWCREST**

"Over 40 varieties, read the label" — public relations spokesperson **TESCO**

Bourbon Biscuits, Coconut Crumble Creams, Crunchy Cookies, Digestive Biscuits, Fruit Shortcake, Ginger Snaps, Ginger Thins, Rich Tea Biscuits, Rich Tea Fingers **WAITROSE**

Fruit Shortcake, Ginger Snaps, Rich Tea, Scrumbles **W. LOW & CO**

breakfast foods

All mueslis **ALARA**

Deluxe Fruit & Nut Muesli **BOOTS**

Mueslis: Goodlife, Goodlife Fruit & Bran, Wholewheat; Bran Flakes, Fruit with Fibre, Sultana Bran, Wheat Flakes, Wholewheat Cereal Biscuits **CO-OP**

Organic Cornflakes **FOODWATCH***

Gluten-Free Muesli **GF DIETARY**

Bran Sticks; *Mueslis:* Alpine, Deluxe, F-Plan Diet, Organic, Rich Fruit **GOODNESS FOODS**

GRANOSE *Mueslis:* 8-Fruit, Bircher, Wholegrain Fruit; Muesli Fritters *(frozen)*

GREEN CITY All mueslis

HAWTHORN VALE *Mueslis:* Crispy, Crunchy, Deluxe, Gluten-Free, High-Fibre, Nutri-Fruit, Triple M

HEALTHRITE Muesli

HOLLAND & BARRETT *Crunchy Cereals:* Caribbean, Bran & Apple, Nutty; *Mueslis:* Deluxe Fruit & Nut, High-Fibre

HOLLY MILL *Bran Breakfast:* Apple & Banana, Toasted Bran Cereal

INFINITY *Mueslis:* Deluxe, Gluten-Free, Organic, Regular

JORDANS *Mueslis:* 4-Grain, Country, Crispy, Deluxe, Fruit & Nut, . Special-Recipe; Multigrain Puffed Cereals, Wholewheat & Raisins

JUST NATURALLY Fruit 'n Flakes

KALLO Puffed Rice

LIFE & HEALTH Sugar-Free Muesli

MAPLETON'S Frugrains

NABISCO Shredded Wheat, Shreddies, Spoon-Sized Shredded Wheat

NISA Wheat Flakes

PREWETT'S *Mueslis:* Bran, Deluxe, Fruit & Nut; Original Date Toasted Fruit & Nut Bran, Wholewheat Flakes

QUAKER Oat Krunchies, Puffed Wheat

food products

35% Fruit & Nut Muesli, Wholewheat Breakfast Biscuits, Wholewheat Flakes	**SAFEWAY**
Mueslis: Deluxe, Wholewheat; High-Fibre Bran, Malted Wheats, Miniwheats, Wheat Flakes, Wholewheat Bisk, Wholewheat Miniflakes	**SAINSBURY**
All mueslis	**SUMA**
Bran Muesli, Wholewheat Cereal, Wholewheat Flakes	**TESCO**
Cereal Biscuits, Wheat Flakes; *Mueslis:* Fruit & Fibre, Fruit & Nut	**WAITROSE**
Bran Breakfast Cereal, Muesli	**WATERMILL**
Cruesli, Weetabix, Weetaflakes	**WEETABIX**
Breakfast Cereals: Almond Crunch, Orange Crunch	**WHOLE EARTH**
Wholewheat Breakfast Biscuits; *Mueslis:* Deluxe, Luxury	**W. LOW & CO**
Frutifort Sugarless Muesli	**ZWICKY**

cakes

Apple & Banana, Carob, Date & Walnut, Orange & Poppyseed	**DOWN TO EARTH**
(sugar-free) Rich Wholefood Fruit Cake	**KITE WHOLEFOODS**
(no added sugar) Apricot Slice, Date Slice, Fruit Slice; Apple Slice, Apricot Crumble Slice, Bread Pudding, Carob Brownies, Date Crumble Slice, Lemon & Poppyseed Cake	**LADYWELL BAKERY**

food products

LINK WHOLEFOODS Fruit Scones

MEG RIVERS* *(no added sugar or fat)* Apricot & Nut Loaf, Date & Nut Loaf; Luxury Nut & Fruit Cake, Rich Nut Cake

WHOLEBAKE FOODS *Slices:* Apricot & Apple, Carob-Coated Pineapple & Almond, Date, Fig, Mince

confectionery

BENDICKS Bitter Mints, Bitter Mocha, Coffee Crisps, Mayfair Mints, Mint Crisps, Orange Crisps, Sporting & Military Chocolate, Victorian Ginger

CO-OP Clear Mints, Fruit Drops, Fruit Jellies, Orange & Lemon Slices, Sugared Almonds

DANIEL QUIGGIN Kendal Mint Cake

DEXTROSOL *Tablets:* Lemon, Original

DORCHESTER CHOCOLATES* Almond Crème, Blackcurrant Crème, Cafe Noix, Carlsbad, Coconut Crème, Coffee Truffle, Crème Suisse, Gooseberry Crème, Hard Caramel, Marzi Noisette, Orange Crème, Orange Crisps, Orange Marzipan, Pineapple, Praline Croquant, Raspberry Crème, Rose Crème, Stem Ginger, Strawberry Crème, Truffle Continental, Truffle Marianne, Turkish Delight. *Gift boxes available with a selection of the above*

DOVE COTTAGE Carob-Coated Fruit Nuggets, Deluxe Carob-Coated Dates, Deluxe Carob-Coated Raisins, Deluxe Carob Mint Leaves

EARTHLORE Assorted *Dairy-Free* Carob Confections,

Hippo Drops *(dairy-free variety)*

Sesame Halva — **ELITE**

Crisp Chocolates: Coffee, Mint, Orange — **ELIZABETH SHAW**

Devon Floral Cachous, Devon Violet Cachous, Gale Force Lozenges, Imps, Pine & Eucalyptus Pastilles; *Sugar-Free Pastilles:* Blackcurrant, Lemon, Orange, Strawberry — **ERNEST JACKSON**

Carob Gold Chocolates, *all varieties*; Seasonal Novelties — **FOODCRAFT**

Assorted Boiled Sweets, Carob Buttons, Chocolate Beans, Mint-Chocolate Beans, Mint Humbugs, Pepermint Rock, Sucrose-Free Boiled Sweets, Sugared Almonds — **FOODWATCH***

Light Carob Drops, Natural-Colour Chocolate Beans — **HAWTHORN VALE**

Dextrose Sweets: Blackcurrant, Lemon, Orange, Raspberry — **INFORM**

Granymels: Caramels, Liquorice, Mint, Orange, Treacle — **ITONA**

Chocolate-Covered Raspberry Ruffles, Ruffle Bar — **JAMESONS**

Parfait Chocolate – Plain *(couverture)* — **LYONS**

After-Dinner Mints, Bitter Chocolate Mints, Chocolate Ginger, Iced Dice, Jelly Beans, Lolli Pops, Marzipan Fruits, Mint Crisp Pieces, Plain Chocolate Thins, Sugared Almonds, Traditional Turkish Delight, Vienna Almonds — **MARKS & SPENCER**

Chocolat Patissier — **MENIER**

NESTLÉ Superfine Plain Chocolate

PANDA Liquorice Cuts; *Bars:* Blackcurrant, Liquorice, Mint Liquorice, Raspberry

PLAMIL *Carob Bars:* Orange, Plain, Roasted Hazelnut; *Chocolate Bars:* Mint, Plain

RITTER *Sport (filled chocolate) Bars:* Marzipan, Peppermint

ROWNTREE MACKINTOSH After-Eight Easter Egg, After-Eight Mints, Black Magic Chocolate Bar; Fox's Glacier Fruits, Fox's Glacier Mints, Fruit Gums, Jellytots, Polo Fruits

SAFEWAY Clear Mints, Jelly Babies, Jelly Drops, Plain-Chocolate Brazil Nuts, Sugared Almonds

SAINSBURY Clear Mints, Fruit Drops Roll Assorted, Fruit Jellies, Jelly Babies, Jelly Beans, Liquorice, Sherbert Cocktail, Soft Mints

TERRY'S Connoisseur's Bitter Chocolate

TESCO Jelly Beans, Liquorice Twists, Sparkling Mints

WAITROSE *Chocolate Bar:* Mint Filling, Strawberry Filling; Chocolate Brazils, Chocolate Ginger, Clear Mints, Fruit Jellies, Jelly Babies, Mint Imperials, Minty Crisp Chocolates, Plain Chocolate, Plain Chocolate Brandy Snap, Plain Chocolate with Hazelnuts

WRIGLEY Doublemint, Juicy Fruit, Spearmint; *Freedent range:* Peppermint, Spearmint; *Hubba Bubba range:* Cola, Pineapple, Tangy Orange; *Orbit (sugar-free) range:* Peppermint, Spearmint; *P.K. range:* Arrowmint,

Blue, Peppermint

Chocolate Brazils, Rainbow Drops *(chocolate discs)*; *After-Dinner Chocolates:* Coffee, Mint, Orange; *Chocolate Thins:* Natural Mint, Orange; *Whirls (chewy sweet):* Liquorice, Toffee

ZOHAR*

confectionery – frozen

Laser Blazer Lolly, Little Menace Orange Lolly

CO-OP

Fresh Juice Orange Maid, Mister Men Water Ice Lollies, Orange Maid, Pineapple Juice Bar, Tropical Juice Bar *(multipack only)*

LYONS MAID

Orange Juice Bars

MARKS & SPENCER

Orange Lolly

SAFEWAY

Orange Lolly *(multipack only)*

SAINSBURY

Jazza, Space Commander, Space Destroyer; *Juicy Lucy range:* Cola, Lemonade, Orange, Raspberry; *Refresher range:* Cider, Cola, Lemonade, Orange

TREATS

Orange Ice Lolly

WAITROSE

Calippo, Orange Frutie, Stick-Up; *Snofruit & Juice range:* Orange & Pineapple; *Sparkles range:* Lemonade, Orangeade

WALL'S

cooking aids

Vegetarian Gravy Mix

APPLEFORD

BISTO	Gravy Powder
BOOTS	TVP *(textured vegetable protein)* Mince, Vegetable Stock
CARABAY	Carrageen Jelly *(instant)*, Carrageen Moss, Dillisk, Irish Kelp Powder, Shredded Dillisk
CLEARSPRING	Tempeh Starter Culture
COMMUNITY FOODS	Agar-Agar Powder
CO-OP	Golden Breadcrumbs, Gravy Browning, Rich Brown Gravy Mix
CRANE SEA VEGETABLES*	Dulse, Kombu, Sea Vegetable Seasoning
CROSSE & BLACKWELL	*Cook-in-the-Pot sauce range:* Beef Goulash, Chicken Chasseur, Chicken Provençale, Chill con Carne, Lamb Ragoût, Madras Curry, Moussaka, Sausage & Tomato Casserole; *Stir-Fry Cook-in-the-Pot sauce range:* Oriental Beef, Sesame & Ginger, Spicy Beef, Sweet & Sour; Gravy Browning
DARENTH VALLEY	Vegetable Stock
DIETADE	Delicia Gravy Mix
DIRECT FOODS	*Protoveg range:* Beef-Style Chunky, Beef-Style Mince, Natural-Style Chunky, Natural-Style Mince, Smokey Snaps
D'SILVA FOODS	Réchard Instant Marinade; *Curry Pastes:* Bafaad, Caldeen, Frithad, Fugaad, Temprade, Vindaloo
ENOLACTO*	Non-Animal Rennet, Yogomagic Natural Yoghurt Starter

Egg Replacer	**ENER-G**
Chocolate Sugar Strands, Egg White Replacer, Gravy Mix, Hundreds & Thous-ands, Jelly Diamonds, Rusk Crumb, Whole Egg Replacer	**FOODWATCH***
Edifas A Egg White Replacer, Low-Protein Egg Replacer	**GF DIETARY**
TVP range: Natural Chunks, Natural Mince, Natural Small Chunks, Savoury Chunks, Savoury Mince	**GOODNESS FOODS**
TSP *(textured soya protein)* Chicken, TVP Chunks	**GRANOSE**
Quick-Jel, *all varieties*	**GREEN'S OF BRIGHTON**
Carob Drops, Dark TVP Mince, Golden Breadcrumbs	**HAWTHORN VALE**
Vegetable Stock	**HEALTHRITE**
Carob Drops	**HIDER**
Savoury Vegetable Concentrate, Yeast Cubes	**HÜGLI**
Caramel-Free Browning	**ITONA**
Naturally Good Gravy Mix	**JESSUP MARKETING**
Wholemeal Breadcrumbs; *Wholemeal Stuffing Mixes:* Chestnut, Hazelnut, Parsley & Thyme, Sage & Onion	**JUST NATURALLY**
Vegetarian Stock Powder	**JUST WHOLEFOODS**

JUVELA   Low-Protein Mix *(gluten-free baking mix)*

KALLO   *Frigg's Stock Cubes:* Onion – Low-Salt, Regular; Tomato, Vegetable – Low-Salt, Regular

KNORR   Vegetable Stock Cubes; *Stuffings:* Apple & Herb, Apricot & Sultana, Cider, Garlic & Herb, Hazelnut & Herb, Sage, Onion and *(synthetic)* Bacon; *Recipe Mixes:* Country Chicken, Sausage Pot

LA ROCHELLE   *Croûtons:* Herb & Garlic, Natural, Wholemeal, Wholemeal Herb & Garlic

LEA & PERRIN'S   Curry Concentrate; *Cooking Sauces:* Chilli & Garlic, Ginger & Orange, Hot Pepper & Lime

LITTLE BEAR   Taco Shells

LOTUS FOODS   All TVP range, Vegetable Rennets

LYONS   Parfait Chocolate – Plain *(couverture)*; Plain Polka Dots

MAHARISHI AYURVEDA*   *Churnas (seasonal herbal mixtures):* Kapha, Pitta, Vata

MAPLETON'S   Agar-Agar

MARIGOLD   Engevita Nutritional Yeast Flakes

MARKS & SPENCER   *Cooking Sauces:* Chilli & Garlic, Peking Barbecue, Sweet & Sour; *Marinades:* American Barbecue, French Herb Quick, Satay Indonesian

MENIER   Chocolat Patissier *(couverture)*

MODERN HEALTH   *Vecon Natural Vegetable Stock:* Easy-Blend *(liquid)*, Original Paste; Gelozone *(jelling agent)*

Concentrated Vegetable Extract, Soya Stock Cubes — **MORGA**

Tempeh Starter Culture — **MURPHY & SON***

Bread Crumbs: Plain, Seasoned; *Croûtons:* Plain, Seasoned; *Stuffing:* Plain, Seasoned; Instant Mashed Potato — **OSEM**

Pastes: Biryani, Green Masala, Kebab, Kashmiri Masala, Madras, Quick Curry (Extra Hot), Quick Curry (Mild), Tandoori, Tikka, Vindaloo Curry — **PATAK'S**

Bread Sauce, Golden Breadcrumbs — **PAXO**

Cooking Sauce Mixes: Beef Bourguignon, Bolognese, Sausage Casserole, Sweet & Sour, Traditional Beef Casserole; *Canned Cooking Sauces:* Chilli, Curry, Sweet & Sour, Tomato Onion; Bread Sauce Mix, Pizza Bases, Vegetable Stock Cubes — **SAFEWAY**

Breadcrumbs, Chocolate Sugar Strands, Deluxe Cooking Chocolate *(plain)*, Hundreds & Thousands, Pizza Base Mix, Plain Chocolate Drops, Plain Chocolate-Flavour Cake Covering, Plain Chocolate Orange-Flavour Cake Covering, Vegetable Purée, Vegetable Stock Tablets; Bread Sauce Mix; *Cooking Sauces:* Chilli, Sweet & Sour — **SAINSBURY**

Genuine Chocolate Shells *(dessert cases)* — **SCHWARTAU**

Carob Drops — **SCOTTS**

Autumn Dulse, Dabberlocks, Fingerware, Grockle, Purple Nori, Sugarware, Summer Dulse — **SEA VEGETABLE CO***

Marinades: American Barbecue Quick, Chilli & Garlic, Classic Chinese, Ginger & — **SHARWOOD'S**

food products

Spring Onion, Indian Spice Quick, Mexican Chilli Quick; *Pastes:* Biryani, Hot Curry, Mild Curry, Tandoori, Vindaloo; Chopped Black Beans, Hoi-Sin Spare Rib Sauce, Yellow Bean Paste

TELMA
Croûtons: Mini Croûtons, Maxi Croûtons; *Stock Cubes:* Mushroom, Onion, Vegetable

TESCO
Cooking Sauce Mixes: Chicken Chasseur, Goulash, Madras Curry; *Mixes:* Bread Sauce, Pizza Base

VEERASWAMY'S
Pastes: Biryani, Hot Curry, Kebab, Medium Curry, Tikka

VICO FOODS
Mr Mash Instant Mashed Potato

WAITROSE
Country Herb Stuffing Mix, Potato Flakes, Wholemeal Breadcrumbs, Vegetable Stock

WESTERN ISLES
Sea Vegetables: Arami, Hijiki, Kombu, Nori, Wakame; Nori Paste Condiment

ZOHAR*
Cake Decorations: Chocolate Vermicelli, Hundreds & Thousands, Jelly Diamonds; *Colours:* Blue, Red, Green, Yellow; *Flavours:* Almond, Vanilla, Rum

cooking fats

ASHLAND
Shredded Vegetable Suet

ATORA
Vegetable Suet

BROADLAND
Shredded Vegetable Suet

CO-OP
Goodlife Cooking Fat, Solid Vegetable Oil

FOODWATCH*
Shredded Vegetable Suet

food products

Nutter, Suenut	**MAPLETON'S**
Trex	**PRINCES**
Solid Vegetable Lard, Vegetable Lard	**PURA**
Solid Vegetable Oil	**SAINSBURY**
White Flora	**VAN DEN BERGH**
Vitaquell Cuisine, Vitaseig	**VITAQUELL**
Pure Solid Vegetable Oil, Shredded Vegetable Suet	**WAITROSE**

cream replacers

Whipped Topping Mix	**FOODWATCH***
On Top Whip Topping, Whip Topping, Whip Topping Base	**RICH'S**
Snowwhip Topping *(frozen)*	**SNOWCREST**

crispbreads etc

Crisproll, Wholemeal Crispbread	**ALLINSON**
Cream Crackers, Oat Rounds, Poppy & Sesame Thins, Scottish Oatcakes, Sesame Seed & Celery Crackers, Wholemeal Thins	**ASDA**
Poppadoms: Garlic, Green Chillies, Plain Madras	**AYESHA**
Finn Crisp Crispbread: Harvest Slims Rye, Harvest Wheat, Light Rye, Original Rye	**BRITANNIA HEALTH**

food products

CARR'S	Table Water Biscuits
CO-OP	Crisp-Bake Cream Crackers, Poppy & Sesame Thins, Savoury Wheat Crackers, Traditional Cream Crackers
COUNTRY BASKET	Organic Rice Cakes, *all varieties*
CRAWFORD'S	Butter Puffs
FOODWATCH*	Sugar-Free Oatcakes
GF DIETARY	Gluten-Free Crackers, Thin Wafers
HAWTHORN VALE	*Sugar-Free Oatcakes:* Coarse, Fine
HEALTHRITE	*Rice Cakes:* No Salt, Sea-Salted
JACOBS	Brown Wheat Crackers, Cream Crackers, High-Bake Water Biscuits
KALLO	All Rice Cakes
KAVLI	Crispbread Wafers, Harvest Crispbread, High-Bake Crispbread, Muesli Crispbread
LIVING FOODS	Organic Rice Cakes, *all varieties*
MARCANTONIO FOODS	Family Pack *(ice cream)* Cones, *(ice cream)* Wafers in Sleeves
MARKS & SPENCER	Bran Crisp Rolls, Butter Puff; *Water Biscuits:* High-Bake, Round
McVITIES	Oatcakes
MILLER'S DAMSEL	*Wheat Wafers:* Celery Seed, Original, Poppy Seed, Sesame Seed
MOLEN AARTJE	*Crispbreads (organic):* Light, Original
NABISCO	Ritz Crackers

Oatcakes: Bran, Fine Highland, Traditional	**NAIRN'S**
Cream Crackers, Savoury Wheat Crackers	**NISA**
Organic Rice Cakes, *all varieties*	**ORGANIC CHOICE**
Sunny Wheat Crispbread, *all varieties*; Cream Crackers, Deli Crackers, Golden Crackers, Sesame Crackers, Wheaten Crackers	**OSEM**
Pappadums: Assorted, Black Peppercorn, Chilli, Garlic, Plain	**PATAK'S**
Oatcakes: Bran, Farmhouse, Rough, Scottish	**PATERSON'S**
Crackers: Hilo, Matzo; *Matzos:* Superfine, Tea, Wheaten	**RAKUSEN**
(gluten-free) High-Fibre Crackers, Low-Protein Crackers	**RITE-DIET**
Crispbreads: High-Fibre, Original, Sesame Seed, Swedish-Style	**RYVITA**
Brown Rye Crispbread, Celery & Sesame Seed Crackers, Oatcakes, Poppy & Sesame Seed Thins, Savoury Wheat Crackers, Water Biscuits	**SAFEWAY**
Butter Puffs, Celery & Sesame Crackers, Cream Crackers, Crisprolls, High-Bake Water Biscuits, Highland Oatcakes, Krispwheat, Light & Crispy Crackers, Oatmeal Bran Biscuits, Wholemeal Krispwheat, Wholemeal Rye Crispbread	**SAINSBURY**
Slymbred: Original, Rye, Sesame, Wholemeal	**SLYMBRAND**
Mazon Crispread: Plain, Superfine	**SNOWCREST**

food products

TESCO	Poppy & Sesame Crackers, Rye Crispbread
VEERASWAMY'S	*Pappadums:* Assorted, Plain
VESSEN	Bran Oatcakes, Wholefood Oatcakes
WAISSEL'S	Gourmet Thins, *all varieties*
WAITROSE	Cream Crackers, High-Bake Water Biscuits, Sesame Crackers
WALKERS	*Oatcakes:* Bran, Crofter's, Fine, Highland
YEHUDA	Matzos

desserts

GRANOSE	*Soya Desserts:* Banana, Chocolate, Strawberry, Vanilla; *Soya Yogerts:* Apricot, Blackcurrant & Apple, Peach Melba, Strawberry
HERA	*Yoga range:* Natural, Raspberry, Strawberry
ITONA	Brown Rice Pudding
JUST WHOLEFOODS	*Vegetarian Jelly Crystals:* Lemon, Strawberry, Tropical Fruits
MARKS & SPENCER	Peach Basket-Weave Pie
NORFOLK PUNCH	Sunday Pudding
OSEM	Instant Puddings, *all varieties*; Quick Jellies, *all varieties*
PLAMIL	*Soya Milk Rice Pudding:* Sugar-Free, Sweetened
PROVAMEL	*Soya Desserts:* Carob, Chocolate, Straw-

berry, Vanilla

Fruit Pies: Apple, Apple Crumb, Blueberry, Cherry, Cherry Crumb, Peach, Rhubarb-Strawberry — **RICH'S**

Ready-to-Eat Jellies: Blackcurrant, Orange, Strawberry — **ROWNTREE'S**

Wholemeal Assorted Fruit Pies — **SAINSBURY**

Vegetarian Chocolate Dessert; *Natural Flavours Jelly Crystals:* 7 varieties; *Vegetarian Jelly Crystals:* 5 varieties — **SNOWCREST**

Yogarts: Black Cherry, Peach Melba, Raspberry, Strawberry — **UNISOY**

Treacle Baked Roll, Wholemeal Dutch Apple Mini-Pies — **WAITROSE**

desserts – frozen

Vive *(non-dairy ice cream)* — **ALLIED FOODS**

Apple & Sultana Sponge Charlotte — **CAPRICORN**

Fruit Sorbets: Lemon, Orange — **CREAMERY FARE**

N'Ice Day (non-dairy ice cream): Hazelnut, Pistachio & Almond, Strawberry, Vanilla — **DAYVILLE**

Real Fruit Lemon Sorbet — **ELITE**

Ice Delight (non-dairy ice cream): Hazelnut, Pistachio & Almond, Raspberry Ripple, Strawberry, Vanilla; *Ice Delight Cones:* Raspberry Ripple, Strawberry, Vanilla — **GENICE**

Lemon Sorbet — **GINO GINELLI**

GRANOSE
Surprise (non-dairy ice cream): Black Cherry, Raspberry Ripple, Tutti-Frutti, Vanilla

LOSELEY
Lemon Sorbet

MARINELLI'S
Ice Supreme (non-dairy ice cream with no added sugar): Chocolate, Raspberry Ripple, Vanilla

McNABS
Soya Ice Cream (single-serve tubs): Fruits of the Forest, Fruits of the Hedgerow, Nuts in May, Pistachio & Almond, Vanilla

PROSPERO FINE ICES
Sorbets: Blackberry with Blackberry Liqueur, Blackcurrant with Cassis, Champagne, Chocolate with Orange and Cointreau, Lemon with Orange, Mango with Grand Marnier, Morello with Kirsch, Passionfruit with Guava, Peach, Raspberry with Raspberry Liqueur, Strawberry with Passionfruit; *Sugar-Free Sorbets:* Blackberry, Blackcurrant, Passionfruit with Guava, Peach, Strawberry

SAINSBURY
Lemon Sorbet

SNOWCREST
Fruit Pies: Apple, Apple Strudel, Apricot, Blackcurrant, Cherry; *Non-Dairy Ice Creams:* Chocolate, Coffee, Coffee Choc Chip, Mint Choc Chip, Orange Choc Chip, Praline, Rum 'n Raisin, Strawberry, Tutti Frutti, Vanilla, Walnut & Chocolate *(Royal range)*; *Non-Dairy Choc Ices:* Vanilla, Vanilla & Strawberry; *Sorbets:* Carnival Cups, Chocolate & Orange, Frosty Caps, Lemon, Orange, Strawberry

SUNRISE
Ice Dream (non-dairy ice cream): Carob, Coconut, Hazelnut, Vanilla, Wild Berry; Carob Ice

THORNE FARM
Fruit Sorbets: Lemon, Orange, Raspberry

Mousses: Carob & Walnut, Fresh Strawberry

VEGEDINE

Fruit Sorbets: Blackcurrant, Lemon, Passion Fruit

WAITROSE

dips & dressings

Mayonnaize range: Garlic, Plain

DIRECT FOODS

Avocado, Garlic, Guacamole, Thousand Is-
lands, Tofu

DUCHESSE

'Naise range: with Garlic, w. Mustard
Seed, w. Peppercorns, w. Tarragon

GREEN DRAGON

Mayonnaise-Style Dressing, Salad Cream-
Style Dressing

LIFE

Soya Dip: with Garlic, w. Peppercorns

MARIGOLD

Mayo range: Garlic & Lemon, Virgin Olive
Oil

MERIDIAN

Soyannaise

RAYNER'S

Avocado dip *(frozen)*

TAL

Lemon & Garlic, Oil-Free Vinaigrette, Thousand Island

WHOLE EARTH

Tofunaise *(organic)*; *Tofu Dips & Dressings*
(organic): Herb, Italian, Mexican

WITTE WONDER

infant foods

Apple Sauce, Apple Sauce & Bananas,
Apple Sauce & Cherries, Apple Sauce &
Pears, Apples & Apricots, Apples & Straw-

BEECH-NUT

berries; Apples, Mandarins & Bananas; Apples, Peach & Strawberries; Apples, Pears & Bananas, Apricots with Pears & Apple Sauce, Bananas w. Tapioca; Bananas, Pears & Apple Sauce; Bananas & Pineapple w. Tapioca; Bartlet Pears; Carrots; Garden Vegetables; Green Beans; Guava; Mango; Mixed Cereal w. Apples & Banana, Mixed Veg. Dinner, Oatmeal w. Apples & Banana; Peaches; Peas; Peas & Carrots, Pears & Pineapple, Plums w. Tapioca, Prunes w. Pears, Rice Cereal w. Apples & Banana; Squash; Sweet Potatoes; *Infant Cereals:* Barley, Mixed Cereals, Oatmeal, Rice

COW & GATE

Fruit & Cereal Breakfast with Vitamin C, Vegetable & Rice Casserole, Vegetable Casserole with Pasta; *Desserts with Added Vitamin C:* Apple, Apple & Banana, Apple & Orange, Cherry Treat, Fruit Delight, Pineapple

FAMILIA

Swiss Baby Food range: Baby Food – Original, Baby Cereal – No Added Sugar

FARLEY'S

Ostersoy Infant Formula

GRANOSE

Carrots & Almond Cream, Mixed Vegetables, Spring Vegetables with 7 Cereals, Spring Vegetables with Brown Rice, Vegetables with Wholemeal Noodles

HEINZ

3–9 Months: Apple with Vitamin C, Banana Dessert with Vitamin C, Fruit & Cereal Breakfast, Fruit Salad; *3–15 months:* Golden Vegetables, Spring Vegetables; Apple & Apricot, Apple & Banana, Apple & Blackcurrant, Apple & Orange, Apple & Pear, Fruit Salad, Just Apple, Mixed Fruit, Pear Cherry; *7–15 months:* Banana Rice & Rosehip Dessert, Fruit Dessert with Tapioca

food products

Baby Rice, Baby Rice with Fruit & Cereals — **MILUPA**

main courses

Vegetable Masala	**BOOTS**
Yellow Pea Pie	**CERES**
Bean Casserole, Kabuli Channa, Lentil & Bean, Mung	**EVERFRESH**
English Shepherd's Pie, Indian Curry, Italian Bolognaise	**FRAMEBORE**
Bean & Mushroom Stew, Chinese Tofu, Goulash, Lentil & Vegetable Casserole, Savoury Pudding, Tofu in Savoury Bean Sauce	**GRANOSE**
Ready-Cook Casserole	**ITONA**
Vegetable Curry	**KATIE'S KITCHEN**
Vegetarian Haggis	**MacSWEENS***
Hawaiian Style, Mushroom Risotto, Pasta & Cabbage, Pasta & Rice, Pasta & Vegetable, Pasta in Tomato Sauce, Rice & Lentil, Risi Bisi, Risotto Milanese, Spanish Paella	**OSEM**
Vegetable Goulash, Wholemeal Cannelloni, Wholemeal Ravioli	**PREWETT'S**
Aloo Gobi, Blackeye Beans, Cabbage Sambhara, Courgette Curry, Curried Chick-Peas, Mixed Vegetable Curry, Mixed Vegetable Pilau, Moong Beans Daal, Peas Pilau Rice, Pilau Rice, Raaj Maahin, Red Lentils Daal, Vegetable Curry & Rice, Yellow Tarka Daal	**SAHIB FOODS**

food products

SAINSBURY   Vegetable Chilli with Cracked Wheat, Vegetable Curry with Spiced Basmati Rice

ST NICHOLAS   Nutty Vegetable Pie

TRIANGLE   Adzuki Nitsuke, Brazilian Bake, Madras Vegetable Sambar

VEGEDINE   Chick-Pea Casserole, Lentil & Zucchini à la Grècque, Mushroom & Nut Terrine, Vegetable & Bean Curry

main courses – frozen

BIRD'S EYE   *Menumaster range:* Sweet & Sour Vegetables with Wild Rice, Vegetable Casserole with Mashed Potato, Vegetable Curry with Pilau Rice

CAPRICORN   Mexican Chilli Bean Ratatouille, Pinto Bean Hot Pot, Vegetarian Cottage Pie

COUNTRY COOKS   Blackeye Bean Bake, Mushroom & Cashew Pilaf, Vegetable Curry

DOWN TO EARTH   Chestnut & Mushroom Roll, Chilli Bean Casserole, Lentil & Vegetable Curry, Shepherdless Pie, Spicy Chick-Peas, Two-Bean Goulash

FRUITS OF THE EARTH   Creamed Coconut Curry, Indonesian Nut Casserole, Mexican Chilli Pancakes, Spinach & Tofu Gnocchi, Sweet & Sour Chick-Peas

GRANOSE   Lentil Dish, Oriental Casserole

GREENE BEANS   Butter Bean & Vegetable Curry, Chick-Pea & Courgette Casserole, Rice with Chick-Peas & Tomatoes, Savoury Mushroom Bake

food products

Spicy Vegetable Chilli	**K.K. WHOLEFOODS**
Bean & Bulgar Wheat Chilli, Lentil Curry, Mixed Bean Shepherd's Pie, Sweet & Sour Kidney Beans, Vegetable Curry, Vegetable Hotpot	**MANGE TOUT FOODS**
Cashew Risotto, Chilli Sin Carne, Sweet & Sour Almonds, Vegetable Goulash	**PAR EXCELLENCE**
Chili Vegeteriani, Mixed Bean Ratatouille, Spicy Garbanzo Beans, Vegetable Curry Rawalpindi	**RESPONSE FOODS**
Aubergine, Cider & Lentil Gratin	**VEGETARIAN CUISINE**
Caribbean Medley, Shepherdess Pie, Spicy Bean Casserole, Vegetable Chilli	**VEGETARIAN FEASTS**

margarines etc

So Good Sunflower Margarine	**DIRECT FOODS**
Milk-Free Margarine	**FOODWATCH***
Diet Half-Fat Spread, Soya Margarine, Sunflower Margarine, VegetableMargarine, Vegetable Margarine – Low Salt	**GRANOSE**
Pure Sunflower Margarine, Pure Vegetable Margarine	**HAWTHORN VALE**
Soya Margarine, Sunflower Margarine	**MERIDIAN**
Vegetable Margarine	**PURE**
Block Margarine, Sunflower Margarine	**RAKUSEN**
Gold Blend	**ROWALLAN CREAMERY**

SAFEWAY	Pure Vegetable Margarine
SD MATTHEWS	DP Pure Margarine
SUMA	Sunflower Margarine
TELMA	Soft Margarine
TOMOR	Block Margarine, Sunflower Low-Fat Spread
VANDEMOORTELE	Vitelma 66
VITAQUELL	Vitaquell Extra, Vitaquell Light, Vitazell *(dietary use)*

mixes – savoury

BE-WELL	*Amazing Grains range:* Cereal Savour, Mixed Grain Vegetable Paella, Sultan's Pilaf, Savoury Couscous; *Easy Beans range:* Bean Stew, Haricot Bean Goulash, Lentil Curry, Spaghetti Bean Bolognese
BOOTS	TVP Burger Mix, TVP Sausage Mix
CO-OP	*Savoury Rices:* Savoury Rices: Mild Curry, Mixed Vegetable
CROSSE & BLACKWELL	*Savoury Rices:* Curried, with Mushrooms, w. Peppers, w. Vegetables
DIETBURGER CO	Dietburger
DIRECT FOODS	5-Grain Burgamix, Burgamix, Chicken-Style Savoury Bake, Jumbo Grills, Lentil & Bean Bake, Minced Soya & Onion Mix, Mr Fritzi Fry's Hawaiian Croquettes, Mr Fritzi Fry's Nutburger, Nut & Grain Bake, Sizzles, Sosmix, Soya Bolognese, Soya Mince with Vegetables

Nut Roast — **ETHOS**

Fantastic Falafil, Nature's Burger, Refried Beans, Tabouli Salad, Tofu Burger, Tofu Scrambler, Vegetarian Chilli — **FANTASTIC FOODS**

Burger Mixes: Lentil, Vegetable — **FOODWATCH***

American Burger Mix — **FRAMEBORE**

Vegetable Rissole Mix — **FRITINI**

Burger Mix — **GOODNESS FOODS**

Burger Mix, Rissolnut, Sausfry; Roasts: Lentil, Mexican Corn, Nut, Sunflower & Sesame — **GRANOSE**

Soysage, Vegetable Bolognese, Vegetable Casserole, Vegetable Chili, Vegetable Curry, Vegetable Goulash, Vegetable Stroganov, Vegetable Stew & Dumplings, Vegetable Supreme — **HERA**

Vegetable Sausage Mix — **JEDWELL FOODS**

Gluten-Free Low-Protein Pizza Mix — **JUVELA**

Soyaberga, Soysos — **LIFE & HEALTH**

Savormix — **MAPLETON'S**

Falafel Mix, Latke Mix — **OSEM**

Chapati, Paratha & Puri Mix; Indian Naan Bread Mix; Onion Bhajia and Pakora Mix; Pilau & Biryani Rice Mix — **PATAK'S**

Vegebanger: Herb, Spicy; *Vegeburger:* Chilli, Herb & Vegetable, No Salt — **REALEAT**

Savoury Rices: Curry, Mushroom & Peppers, Spanish — **SAFEWAY**

SAINSBURY	Savoury Tomato Rice
TELMA	Fallafel Mix, Matzo Ball Mix
TESCO	*Savoury Rices:* Golden, Hot Curry, Mild Curry, Mixed Vegetable, Tomato
TOMORROW FOODS	*Cutlet Mixes:* Aduki Bean Loaf, Dhal & Chapatti, Mexican, Nut, Tandoori

mixes – sweet

CO-OP	Rock Cake Mix
FOODWATCH*	Frozen Dessert Mix; *'S' Creem (non-dairy ice cream) range:* Carob, Strawberry, Vanilla; *Dessert Mixes:* Carob, Chocolate; *Whip Mixes:* Apricot Dessert, Blackcurrant Dessert, Strawberry Dessert
GRANOSE	*Wholemeal Cake Mixes:* Banana, Coconut, Date & Walnut, Orange, Sultana & Ginger
GREEN'S OF BRIGHTON	Carmel Dessert Mix, Crunchy Crumble Mix
NESTLÉ	Nesquick, *all varieties*
NUTWOOD	*Instant Drink Mixes:* Carob-Hazelnut, Choco-Hazelnut
PREWETT'S	*Ice Cream Mixes:* Carob, Strawberry, Vanilla
TESCO	Rock Cake Mix

pastry

CERES	Pastry Cases, Wholemeal pastry

food products

Fillo Pastry, Puff Pastry Blocks, Shortcrust Pastry Blocks, Sweet Shortcrust Pastry Blocks, Vol-au-Vent, Wholemeal Puff Pastry, Wholemeal Shortcrust Pastry
JUS-ROL

Wholemeal Puff Pastry
GREENROSE FOODS

Wholemeal Shortcrust Pastry
LOSELY PARK FARMS

Wholemeal Pastry Cases *(unsweetened)*
PREWETT'S

Puff pastry *(fresh and frozen)*, Shortcrust Pastry *(fresh and frozen)*, Vol-au-Vent Cases
SAINSBURY

Vegetable Puff Pastry, Vegetable Shortcrust Pastry
SNOWCREST

Puff Pastry, Shortcrust Pastry
WAITROSE

pet foods

Happidog Dog Food *(canned and dried)*; Bunny Blend Rabbit Food, Golden Choice Hampster, Gerbil and Mice Food
HAPPIDOG*

Wafcol Vegetarian *(dog food)*
WAFCOL*

Dog Meal
WATERMILL*

savouries

Tofu Burgers: Chilli, Savoury, Vegetable
CAULDRON

Baked Beans in Reduced Sugar and Salt Tomato Sauce, Baked Beans in Tomato Sauce, Spaghetti in Reduced Sugar and Salt Tomato Sauce, Spaghetti in Tomato Sauce, Spaghetti Numbers in Tomato Sa-
CO-OP

...uce, Spaghetti Rings in Tomato Sauce, Wholewheat Spaghetti in Tomato Sauce

CROSSE & BLACKWELL

Alphabetti Spaghetti, Baked Beans in Tomato Sauce, Fred Bear – Beans & Pasta Shapes, Spaghetti Saurus, Straight-Cut Spaghetti, Treasure Island, Wholewheat Spaghetti; *Healthy Balance range:* Beans in Tomato Sauce, Higher-Fibre Spaghetti in Tomato Sauce

EASTERN NATURAL FOODS

Tofu Burgers: Chilli, Herb, Tomato

GF DIETARY

Low-Protein Gluten-Free Vegetable Burgers in Barbeque Sauce

GOODLIFE

Bean Bangers: Herb, Spicy; Cutlets: Mexican, Nut, Tandoori, Vegetable & Sesame; Bean Bites, Falafel, Tofu Satay, Vegetable Kofta

GRANOSE

Bologna, Meatless Savoury Cuts, Mock Duck, Nutbrawn, Nut Loaf, Nuttolene, Sausalatas, Saviand, Tender Bits, Vege-cuts, Vegelinks

HEINZ

Baked Beans with Tomato Sauce, Curried Beans with Sultanas; *Weight Watchers range:* No-Added-Sugar Baked Beans

HERA

Okara Patties, Savoury Tofu Burgers, Spicy Tofu Burgers

HÖFEL'S

Vegetable Curries: Mild, Medium-Hot, Vindaloo

HOLLAND & BARRETT

Lentil Dhal, Mexican Style Red Kidney Beans, Mild Vegetable Curry, Vindaloo Hot Vegetable Curry

HP

Baked Beans; *Healthy Choice range:* Baked Beans

Refried Beans	**LITTLE BEAR**
Beans in Tomato Sauce, Spaghetti in Tomato Sauce	**LITTLEWOOD'S**
Nut Luncheon Roll; *Rissols:* in Brown Sauce, in Tomato Sauce	**MAPLETON'S**
Chinese Mixed Vegetables, Ratatouille	**MARKS & SPENCER**
Baked Beans, Spaghetti in Tomato Sauce	**NISA**
Pease Pudding	**PLAMIL**
Baked Beans	**RAKUSEN**
Baked Beans, Curried Beans, Low-Salt/Low-Sugar Baked Beans, Mixed Bean Salad in Spicy Sauce, Ratatouille, Spaghetti in Tomato Sauce, Spaghetti Rings in Tomato Sauce	**SAFEWAY**
Baked Beans Reduced Salt & Sugar, Barbecued Beans, Beans in Tomato Sauce, Chilli Beans in Chilli Sauce, Curried Beans, Mixed Beans in Spicy Pepper Sauce	**SAINSBURY**
Mild Vegetable Curry, Mexican Beans	**SIMPSON'S**
Beans in Tomato Sauce	**SMEDLEY**
Beans in Tomato Sauce, Chilli Beans	**TESCO**
Baked Beans, Mixed-Bean Salad in Tomato Sauce, Mixed Bean Salad in Vinaigrette	**TRIANGLE**
3-Minute Chinese Fried Rice, 3-Minute Mild Curry Rice	**UNCLE BEN'S**

food products

WAITROSE   Baked Beans in Tomato Sauce, Baked
Beans in Tomato Sauce with No Added
Sugar/Starch, Spaghetti in Tomato Sauce,
Swiss-Style Potato Fry, Pepper Salad,
Ratatouille

WATERFALL FOODS   Satay Sticks; *Savoury Soyfu Nuggets:*
Garlic & Tomato, Provençale, Satay, Soyfu,
Sweet & Sour, Tikka; *Vegelami Slice:*
Paprika, Pepper, Turmeric & Chestnut

WHOLE EARTH   Baked Beans, Organic Baked Beans, Organic Brown Rice and Vegetables

savouries – fresh

CERES   *Pasties:* Curried Vegetable, Mushroom &
Potato, Yellow Pea & Vegetable; Nut
Rissoles

CO-OP   *Salads:* 3-Bean, Carrot, Nut & Sultana

LADYWELL BAKERY   *Pasties:* Curry, Mexican Bean, Mushroom,
Spinach & Potato, Winter Vegetable; Nut-
meat Rolls

LIFECYCLE   *(takeaway)* Falafel, Mexican Bean Slice,
Onion Bhaji, Pakora, Soyasos Roll, Veg-
etable Pasty, Vegetable Samosa

LINK WHOLEFOODS   Aduki Burgers, Curry Puff, Rice & Chilli
Pie, Savoury Vegetables, Vegetable Saus-
ages

LITTLEWOOD'S   White Rice with Carrot/Sultana, White Rice
with Pepper; *Salads:* Carrot & Nut, Italian
Pasta, Mexican Bean, Mexican Rice

MARKS & SPENCER   *Salads:* Carrot & Nut, Mexican-Style Bean,
Rice and Wholefood; Onion Bhaji, Rata-
touille; Gazpacho Soup

Salads: 5-Bean, Carrot & Nut, Trimrite Vegetable; Basmati Rice, Vegetable Chilli, Vegetable Pie *(individual)*, Vegetable Ratatouille, Vegetable Rogan Josh
SAFEWAY

Onion Bhaji, Pakora, Potato Vegetable Cutlet, Vegetable Samosa, Vegetable Spring Roll
SAHIB FOODS

Salads: Brown Rice, Crisp Vegetable; Courgette Provençale, Fresh Vegetable Pasty, Gobi Aloo Sag, Mild Curried Rice, Onion Bhaji, Ratatouille, Vegetable Samosa
SAINSBURY

Felafel, Onion Bhaji, Spinach Spring Roll, Vegetable Pakora, Vegetable Samosa, Vegetable Spring Roll, Wholemeal Vege-table Samosa
SULTAN'S TABLE

Mixed Vegetable Curry, Vegetable Chilli
TESCO

Salads: 5-Bean, Beansprout, Beansprout & Chick-Pea, Brown Rice, Carnival, Carrot & Nut, Fresh Bean, Fresh Continental, Fresh 6-Vegetable, Fresh Spinach, Harvest Salad in Orange Dressing, Jardinière, Leek & Bean, Lentil, Mexican Bean, Mixed Cabbage & Walnut, Spicy Bean Salad, Spring, Sunrise, Turmeric Rice, Wild Rice; Bubble & Squeak, Chinese Leaf & Sweetcorn, Mushrooms à la Grècque, Onion Bhaji, Onion & Spinach Bhaji, Pakora, Pilau Rice, Ratatouille, Rice à la Grècque, Spring Roll, Stir Fry, Tabouleh, Tahinosalata, Vegetable Curry, Vegetable Samosa
WAITROSE

savouries – frozen

Crunchy Potato Grill; *Vegetable Rice range:*
BIRD'S EYE

American Recipe, Chinese Recipe

DIETBURGER CO — Dietburger

DOWN TO EARTH — Bean & Vegetable Pasty, Nutmeat Roll, Samosa; *Burgers:* Millet, Sunflower Seed

EAT HEALTHY PRODUCTS — *Patties:* Chinese, Lentil & Rice, Mexicaine, Mixed Nut, Mixed Vegetable, Tandoori

GRANOSE — *Burgers:* Celery, Nut & Sesame; Vegetarian Sausages

GREENROSE FOODS — Curried Vegetable Pie, Savoury Vegetable Pasty, Savoury Vegetable Roll

MARKS & SPENCER — Potato Waffles

PUKKA PIES — Vegetable & Tofu Pie with Wholemeal Puff Pastry

ROSS — Bubble & Squeak, Hash Browns, Oven Crunchies, Potato Croquettes, Potato Waffles; *Vegetable Mixes:* Indian Special Rice, Ratatouille, Rice Mix

SAFEWAY — Breaded Onion Rings, Potato Waffles

SAINSBURY — Vegetable Rolls *(party-size)*

ST NICHOLAS — Vegetable Samosas

SULTAN'S TABLE — Felafel

SUNRISE — *Tofu & Vegetable Pies:* Celery & Peppers, Chinese Vegetables, Ratatouille; Vegetarian Quarter-Pound Burgers

VEGETARIAN'S CHOICE — Burgers, Sausages

VEGETARIAN FEASTS — *Feastburgers:* Chilli, Savoury; Great Grain Burgers

Burgers: Chilli, Nut, Veggie; *Sosages:* Savoury, Veggie	**VEGGIES**
Bombay Aloo, Flat Onion Bhaji, Potato & Onion Bhaji, Spinach Pakora, Vegetable Samosa	**WEST LONDON FOODS**

savoury sauces

Ragu: with Green & Red Peppers, w. Sliced Mushrooms, w. Onions & Garlic, Traditional-Style	**BROOKE BOND/OXO**
Prego Sauces: Pizza Topping, Sauce for Bolognese; Tomato & Mushroom Spaghetti Sauce	**CAMPBELL**
Pasta Sauces: Tomato & Mixed Herb, Tomato & Mushroom, Tomato, Onion & Garlic, Tomato & Peppers	**CIRIO**
Bonne Cuisine range: Bolognese Sauce; *Pasta Choice range:* Napolitan	**CROSSE & BLACKWELL**
Napoletana Sauce, Vegetale Sauce; Napoletana Sauce *(chilled)*	**DOLMIO**
Satay Sauce, Smokey BBQ Sauce	**DUCHESSE**
Basil Sauce, Sauce Bolognese	**FLORENTINO**
Italian Sauce, Mexican Sauce, Spanish Sauce	**GRANOSE**
Spagheroni Pasta Sauce	**HEINZ**
Tartare Sauce, Worcestershire Sauce	**LIFE**
Horseradish Sauce	**MRS ELSWOOD**
Greek Sauce, Mushroom Sauce, Spaghetti Sauce, Tangy Roast Sauce	**OSEM**

food products

PATAK'S   Delhi Curry (Mild), Madras Curry (Hot), Rogan Josh Curry, Vindaloo Curry (Extra Hot)

PREWETT'S   Curry Ketchup

SAFEWAY   Pasta Sauce

SAINSBURY   Classic Italian, Classic Italian with Mushrooms, Classic Italian with Peppers, Italian Tomato, Napolitana

SANTINI   *Pasta Sauces:* Marettimo, Pomodoro, Sicilianio, Veronese

SHARWOOD'S   A1 Fruity, Curry, Chutney, Extra Hot Vindaloo, Hot Madras, Medium Dhansak, Medium Rogan Josh

TELMA   Tehina Sauce

TESCO   Napolitana

VEERASWAMY'S   Delhi Mild Curry, Korma Curry, Madras Hot Curry, Moglai Medium Curry, Rogan Josh Curry, Vegetable Curry (Hot), Vegetable Curry (Mild), Vindaloo Curry

WHOLE EARTH   Italiano, Kensington Sauce

ZEST FOODS   Pesto – *Vegan*

seasonal foods

CO-OP   Traditional Christmas Pudding

EARTHLORE   Carob Easter Eggs – *Dairy-Free*; Carob Seasonal Novelties *(dairy-free varieties)*

FOODCRAFT   Seasonal Novelties

Spiced Fruit Filling *(mincemeat alternative)*	**FOODWATCH***
Christmas Pudding	**GRANOSE**
Beanmilk Chunky Egg	**ITONA**
(all sugar-free) Brandy Mince Fruit *(mincemeat)*, Christmas Cake, Christmas Pudding	**KITE WHOLEFOODS**
No-Added-Sugar Mincemeat, Suet-Free Mincemeat	**MERIDIAN**
Christmas Pudding, Mincemeat	**NORFOLK PUNCH**
After-Eight Easter Egg	**ROWNTREE MACKINTOSH**

snacks – savoury

Sesame Sticks	**COMMUNITY FOODS**
Flavoured Crisps: Salt & Vinegar; Onion Rings, Salt & Vinegar Chipsnacks	**CO-OP**
Fantastic Noodles: Curry Vegetable, Miso Vegetable, Tomato Vegetable	**FANTASTIC FOODS**
Flavoured Crisps: Tomato Sauce; Pot Chilli, Pot Noodle – Spicy Curry, Pot Rice – Chicken Curry	**GOLDEN WONDER**
Flavoured Crisps: Sea Salt & Cider Vinegar	**HEDGEHOG**
Japanese Rice Crackers, Shanghai Nuts, Tainan Mix	**HIDER**
Flavoured Crisps: Beef, Worcester Sauce; *Flavoured Discos:* Beef, Salt & Vinegar;	**KP FOODS**

Hula Hoops: Ready-Salted, Savoury Onion; *Flavoured Mini-Chips:* Barbecue; *Flavoured Dry-Roast Peanuts:* Oriental Spice, Salt & Vinegar; Barbecue-Flavour Skips, Popadoms

LITTLE BEAR

Bearitos: Blue Corn Salted, Tortilla Chips, Yellow Corn No Salt, Yellow Corn Salted

MARKS & SPENCER

Flavoured Crisps: Natural Salt & Vinegar; Croutons, Italian-Style Pizza Bits, Mexican-Style Tortilla Chips, Salt & Vinegar Chiplets

MEXI-SNAX

Tortilla Chips (organic): Blue Corn, No Salt, Salted

MOLEN AARTJE

Potato Chips (organic): Paprika, Salt

OSEM

Tintins: Onion & Garlic, Plain; *Bissli range:* Falafel, Bar-b-Q, Onion, Onion & Garlic, Smokey, Taco; *Croutons:* Mini Mandels, Maxi Mandels; Bamba, MiniPretzels, Popco, Rice Crackers, Snack Tidbits, Soup Tidbits

PATAK'S

Bombay Mix, Cobras, Chevda, Mexican Mix, Pythons, Rattlers

PHILEAS FOGG

Mignons Morçeaux, Tortilla Chips

SAFEWAY

Flavoured Crispy Squares: Salt & Vinegar; *Flavoured Crunchy Sticks:* Salt & Vinegar

SAINSBURY

Les Mignons, Potato Rings, Potato Squares, Potato Triangles, Tortilla Chips

TESCO

Flavoured Crisps: Salt & Vinegar; *Flavoured Crunchy Sticks:* Salt & Vinegar; *Flavoured Potato Chips:* Salt & Vinegar; Onion Rings, Potato Triangles

VESSEN

Snacks range: Herb Pâté, Mushroom Pâté, Pepper Pâté

Flavoured Crisps: Lower-Fat Salt & Vinegar, Lower-Fat Spring Onion, Salt & Vinegar; Onion Rings, Potato Rings, Salt & Vinegar Potato Twirls, Salt & Vinegar Savoury Sticks — **WAITROSE**

Flavoured Crisps: Beef & Onion, Kashmir Mild Poppadum-Style; Salt & Vinegar French Fries — **WALKER'S**

Pasta Pots: Garden Vegetable, Napoli, Pesto, Savoury Noodle — **WHOLE EARTH**

Cartwheels (crunchy potato snack): Natural, Mexican Spice, Salt & Vinegar — **ZOHAR***

snacks – sweet

Cookies: Fruit & Nut, Oatmeal & Raisin, Tropical Coconut — **BARBARA'S BAKERY**

Fruit Bars (sugar-free): Apricot, Coconut, Date, Fig, Nuts, Prune, Raisin, Sesame — **CASTUS**

Flapjack, Wholemeal Fruit Slice — **COUNTRY FITNESS**

Halvas: with Chocolate, w. Nut, w. Pistachios, w. Vanilla — **CYPRESSA**

Carob-Coated Bars: Fruit, Muesli Pineapple; Fruit Bread — **GRANOSE**

Kiwi Fruit Snack — **HANSELLS**

No-Added-Sugar Bars: Apple & Cardamom, Apricot & Almond — **HOLLY MILL**

Bars: Beanmilk Chunky, Beanmilk Nutty, Oranges & Lemons — **ITONA**

Flapjack: Wholewheat, Wholewheat Fruit — **KIPPAX**

food products

LA ROCHELLE Mr Wilkinson's Stoneground Wholemeal-Flour Eccles Cakes

LUCY FOODS *Ra Bars:* Fruit, Nut

PATERSON'S *Giant Cookies:* Choc Chip, Fruit, Jumbo Oat

PLAMIL *Carob-Coated Fruit & Nut Bar:* Apple, Apricot, Pear

RITE-DIET *Crunchy Bar (gluten-free):* Carob, Fruit 'n Nut

SHEPHERDBOY Multifruit Bar; *Fruit & Nut Bars:* Apple, Bran, Carob, Coconut, Ginger, Sunflower, Tangy; *Just So range:* Crispy Carob, Carob with Ginger, Carob w. Orange, Carob w. Peppermint

VICO FOODS Apple Crackles

WAITROSE *Popcorn:* Caramel Peanut, Chocolate Mint, Chocolate

WILCOX & LOMER *Fig Cakes:* Apricot & Almond, Raisin & Coconut, Spiced Walnut & Ginger, Traditional Spanish

soups

BOOTS Bean & Pepper, Country Vegetable, Potato & Leek, Spicy Vegetable, Vegetarian Green Bean, Vegetarian Thick Lentil, Vegetarian Thick Potato

CAMPBELL'S *Condensed range:* Golden Vegetable, Tomato, Vegetable; *Granny's range:* Vegetable, Winter Vegetable; *Bumper Harvest range:* Vegetable; *Soup in a Glass range:* Tomato Italienne

Garden Vegetable, Harvest Thick Vegetable; *Chunky Soups:* Tomato & Vegetable, Vegetable; *Healthy Balance range:* Garden Vegetable, Harvest Thick Vegetable; *Box Soups:* Minestrone, Spring Vegetable

CROSSE & BLACKWELL

(all frozen) Bean & Barley, Beetroot, Chunky Vegetable, Leek & Potato, Lentil & Spinach, Lentil & Tomato

GREENE BEANS

Big Soups range: Vegetable; *Ready-to-Serve range:* Vegetable; *Weight Watchers range:* Vegetable; *Whole Soups range:* Farmhouse Vegetable, Lentil, Tomato & Lentil, Winter Vegetable

HEINZ

Dried: Farmhouse Vegetable, Lentil & Bean, Minestrone, Vegetable Goulash

HERA

Cubes: Mushroom Broth, Onion, Tomato; *Packet:* Tomato Soup; Vegetable Broth Granules

HÜGLI

Crofter's Thick Vegetable, Florida Spring Vegetable

KNORR

Spring Vegetable, Thick Vegetable, Vegetable

LITTLEWOODS

Instant Vegetable Broth Mix

MORGA

Cubes: Beef Parve *(instant)*, Mushroom, Vegetable, Clear Seasoned Broth; *Instant:* Onion, Minestrone, Mushroom, Pea with Croûtons, Tomato & Vegetable, Vegetable with Croûtons; *Gourmet Cuisine range:* French Onion, Minestrone, Mushroom, Noodle Mix, Spring Vegetable; *Gourmet Cuisine – Instant range:* Chicken-Flavour Noodle, French Onion with Croûtons, Mushroom with Croûtons, Spring Vegetable with Croûtons; *Twin Pack range:*

OSEM

food products

Alef Bet, Asparagus, Celery, Continental Mushroom, Country Vegetable, Garden Vegetable, Green Pea, Minestrone, Mushroom, Mushroom Barley, Noodle Mix, Onion, Potato & Mixed Vegetable, Spring Vegetable, Tomato, Tomato & Rice

RAKUSEN
Vegetarian Cuisine range: Dutch Pea, Spanish Lentil, Thick Winter, Tomato & Rice, Tuscan Bean

REALEAT
Honest to Goodness (instant) range: Onion, Mulligatawny, Tomato

SAFEWAY
Canned: Country Vegetable, Gazpacho, Minestrone; *Dried:* French Onion, Minestrone; *Instant:* Minestrone, Slim Soup *(tomato)*

SAINSBURY
Canned: Extra Thick Vegetable, Gazpacho, Tomato, Vegetable; *Dried:* French Onion, Spring Vegetable; *Instant:* French Onion

SUMA
Complete Vegetable Soup Mix

TELMA
Instant Borscht; *Express Instant Cream range:* Asparagus, Corn, Mushroom, Onion, Vegetable; *Low-Calorie range:* Onion, Tomato; *Twinpack range:* Asparagus, Krupnick, Mushroom, Onion, Vegetable

TESCO
French Onion, Spring Vegetable, Thick Vegetable, Vegetable

TRIANGLE
Vegetable Soup

VEERASWAMY'S
Mulligatawny Soup

WAITROSE
French Onion, Low-Calorie Vegetable, Spring Vegetable, Tomato Soup

Instant Miso Soup **WESTERN ISLES**

soya bean products

Tofu: Marinated, Original, Smoked **CAULDRON FOODS**

Tofu **EASTERN NATURAL FOODS**

Tempeh, Tofu **FULL OF BEANS**

Tofeata Tofu **HERA**

Tempeh **IMPULSE FOODS**

Tofu: Braised, Hi-Protein, Marinated **MARIGOLD**

Tofu: Firm, Silken **MORI-NU**

Dried Tofu **WESTERN ISLES**

soya milks

Soya Milk **BOOTS**

Soya Milk Powder **GOODNESS FOODS**

Sugar-Free, Sweetened; *Organic:* Sugar-Free; *Flavoured:* Banana, Carob, Coconut, Strawberry; Soyagen Soya Milk Powder **GRANOSE**

Sugar-Free, Sweetened **HOLLAND & BARRETT**

Nature Wise Soya Milk **LANCASHIRE DAIRIES**

Concentrated Sugar-Free, Concentrated Sweetened, Mini-Pots *(sugar-free),* Ready- **PLAMIL**

	to-Use Sugar-Free, Ready-to-Use Sweetened
PROVAMEL	*Organic:* Sugar-Free, Sweetened
SAFEWAY	Sugar-Free, Sweetened
SOJAL	Soya Milk
SUNRISE	Sugar & Salt-Free, Sugar-Free, Sweetened; *Organic:* with Malt, with Sugar; *Flavoured:* Banana, Chocolate, Strawberry
TESCO	Sugar-Free, Sweetened
UNISOY	Gold, White Wave Sugar-Free, White Wave Sweetened; *Flavoured:* Carob & Banana Organic
WAITROSE	Soya Milk
WESTERN ISLES	Bonsoy

spreads – savoury

BOOTS	Savoury Spread
CAULDRON	*Pâtés:* Mushroom, Smoked Tofu, Tomato & Red Pepper
CHALICE FOODS	Kalamata Olive Pâté, Peanut & Raisin Butter, Savoury Peanut Butter (with spices)
CLAREMONT CHEESE CO	*Vegese range:* Garlic, Onion & Chives, Plain, Smoked Hickory
DOWN TO EARTH	Creole Pâté, Pinto Pâté
DUCHESSE	Sandwich Spread
FLORENTINO	Garlic Spread, Pizza Spread

Apple & Onion Spread, Tastex, Vegetable Pâté; *Vegetarian Spreads:* Herb, Mushroom, Tomato	**GRANOSE**
Scheese range: Cheddar, Smoked Gouda	**GREEN DRAGON**
Fromsoya	**KALLO**
Hazelnut & Lentil Pâté *(frozen)*	**K.K. WHOLEFOODS**
Golden Harvest Vegetable Pâté	**LEISURE**
Soyacheese: Plain, Smoky	**MARIGOLD**
Veeze range: No Added Flavour, with Added Garlic	**PLAMIL**
Savoury Spread	**SAFEWAY**
Vegetable Pâté	**TELMA**
Vegetable Pâtés: Chestnut, Hazelnut, Spicy Bean	**UNICORN FOODS**
Organic Vegetarian Pâtés: Carrot, Chestnut, Chick-Pea, Fig, Hazelnut, Mushroom, Onion, Provençe	**URD**
Pâtés: Herb, Mushroom, Pepper; *Tartex range:* Herb, Mushroom, Pepper, Plain	**VESSEN**
Satay Spread: Hot & Spicy, Standard	**WATERFALL FOODS**
Savoury Bean, Spicy Spread, Tasty Tomato	**WILLIAM'S FAVOURITE**
Tofu Sandwich Spreads (organic): Celery, Dill, Garlic, Mushroom, Paprika	**WITTE WONDER**

spreads – sweet

Rose Petal Conserve	**MAHARISHI AYURVEDA***

MERIDIAN	Caronut
MOLEN AARTJE	*Carobella (organic):* Hazelnut, Orange, Original
NUTWOOD	Carob-Hazelnut Spread
OSEM	Chocolate Flavour, Chocolate with Hazelnuts
PLAMIL	*Carob Spread:* Sugar-Free, Sweetened
SAINSBURY	Chocolate Spread
SNOWCREST	Chocky Nut Spread, Chocolate Spread

whiteners

CoffeeMate *(kosher parve sachet version)*, ParevMate

The range of producers at home and abroad and the number of UK and imported alcoholic drinks are so great as to warrant a publication of their own to fully catalogue even that fraction whose production is free of animal involvement. The brief observations that follow should therefore be regarded as merely an introduction to a massive, and at times highly complex, subject.

The use of animal products in the alcohol industry, predominantly as clearing (clarifying) agents, but also as colourants — e.g. cochineal (E120) in Campari, can be compared with the use of gelatine by the photographic industry. That is, the products are readily available, they 'work' and so they continue to be used out of habit. Recent and imminent developments in gelatine-free film technology parallel the progress made by brewers with filtration of most keg, bottled and canned beers, ending their once-total reliance upon animal derivatives for certain processes.

To take another aspect of alcohol-related animal abuse, alcohol is, quite ludicrously, tested on non-human animals (3,746 in the UK in 1987 — the latest available figures at the time of writing). Such experimentation is not brand-related and so falls into the same category as, say, water and other age-old, seemingly innocuous substances, quantities of which have, at one time or another, been forced into animals in the name of 'research'.

beers As a general rule of thumb, which the reader may

wish to use when considering a brand not listed below, beers can be roughly classified into two categories: one, the traditional cask-conditioned, sediment beers — which will have used isinglass finings (obtained from the air bladders of certain fish) to clear them; and two, the canned, bottled and keg beers — which will have been filtrated instead.

There are exceptions to this 'rule', however. For instance, both *Guinness* and *Scottish & Newcastle* report that (animal-derived) finings are used in *all* of their beers.

spirits Enquiries continue to show that the production of whisky, brandy, gin, Pernod, rum and vodka does not entail the use of any animal-derived agents or ingredients, although readers may be interested to learn that the main, protein-rich by-products of scotch whisky production are pelletized and sold to farmers to enrich cattle feed.

wines Whilst the principal ingredients of all wines are obviously of vegetable origin, animal derivatives are often used for fining (clarifying) or other purposes. Animal products used in the various stages of production can include: gelatine, bone marrow, isinglass, egg albumen, milk, milk casein, dried blood and fish oil. Alternative, non-animal, fining agents include powdered limestone, special clays like bentonite and kieselguhr, vegetable plaques and liquid plant casein.

The lists in the following pages have been compiled on the basis of assurances that the products contain no animal derivatives, and that no such derivatives were used in their processing, fermenting, brewing, clearing or colouring. Please note that low-alcohol drinks, where available, appear at the end of a company's entry.

alcoholic beverages

beers & ciders

ALLIED BREWERIES

National: Long Life [can/keg], Lowenbrau Diat Pils [bottle/can], Lowenbrau Strong Lager [can/keg], St. Christopher [bottle]; *South:* Barleycorn Pale Ale [keg], Benskins Pale Mild [keg], Friary Meux Light Ale [bottle], Taylor Walker Light Ale [bottle]; *North:* Falstaff [keg], Imperial [keg], Tetley Heavy [keg], Tetley Special Pale Ale [bottle]; *Scotland:* Alloa Export Ale [keg], Alloa Original Light [keg], Alloa Special 70/- [can/keg], Alloa Sweet Stout [bottle], Arrols 80/- Ale [bottle/can], Dryborough's Best Scotch [keg], Dryborough's Heavy [keg], Scottish Pride Lager [can]

ASPALL CYDER HOUSE

Still Medium Sweet and Still Dry Cyders

GEORGE BATEMAN & SON

India Pale Ale [bottle], Keg Bitter, Nut Brown [bottle], Victory Ale [bottle]

BODDINGTONS BREWERIES

Higsons Brewery Conditioned Bitter, Higsons Brewery Conditioned Mild, Higsons Double Top, Kaltenberg Braumeister Lager

BURTONWOOD BREWERY

Best Bitter [keg/can], Dagen Lager [can], Dark Milk [keg], Special Pale [keg/bottle], Strait [keg], Super Brown Ale [bottle], Tom Forshaws Bitter [can], Top Hat [keg/bottle]; Strait Low Alcohol Beer

CORNISH BREWERY CO

Cornish Light Ale, Cornish Brown Ale, Cornish Saxon, Export Gold Lager; *Newquay Steam Beer Range:* Extra Bitter, Extra Brown, Extra Lager, Extra Stout, Keg Bitter, Keg Stout, Keg Pils, Pils, Strong Bitter, Strong Brown, Strong Lager, Strong Pils, Strong Stout, XXX Lager; Prohibition Lager (Low Alcohol)

alcoholic beverages

COUNTRYMAN CIDER

All products

COURAGE

Foster's Lager [can], Kronenbourg Lager [can and draught]

FULLER, SMITH & TURNER

Bitter [keg/can], Brown Ale [bottle], ESB Export, Golden Pride [bottle/can], K2 Lager [keg/can], London Pride [bottle/keg/can], Pale Ale [bottle], Mild [keg]

GABRÜDES GATZWEILER

Gatzweilers Alt Beer [bottle and keg]; Gatz Alcoholfrei [bottle]

GLENNY BREWERY*

Hobgoblin, Witney Bitter, Wychwood Best Bitter *(animal-free versions direct from brewery only)*

GREENE, KING & SONS

Brewers Bitter; Clausthaler Special Low Alcohol Lager (Binding Brauerei AG/Surfax Ltd); Lowes Low Alcohol Bitter

HALL & WOODHOUSE

Best Bitter [keg/can], Brock Lager [keg], Export Bitter [keg], Hofbrau Export Lager [keg], Malthouse Bitter [keg/can], Oasthouse Bitter [can], Royal Hofbrau Lager [keg], Skona Lager [can], Stingo Strong Beer [bottle]; Badger Low Alcohol Bitter

JOSEPH HOLT

Brown Stout

JENNINGS BROTHERS

Traditional Bitter, Traditional Mild, Castle Keg Bitter, Castle Keg Mild, Cambrian Ale [bottle]

KING & BARNES

J.K. Lager

MACLAY & CO

All keg beers (Export, Special & Pale Ale)

MARSTON, THOMPSON & EVERSHED

Pilsner Lagerbier

alcoholic beverages

Farmers Ale [bottle], Golden Mild [draught], **McMULLEN & SONS**
Hartsman Lager [draught/can], Steingold
Export Lager [draught], No.1 - Draught
Bitter; Crafter Low Alcohol Bitter [draught
only]

Kaltenberg Braumeister Lager **MORLAND & CO**

Friars Ale [keg], Harp Extra Lager, Varsity **MORRELLS**
Keg **BREWERY**

Dark Star naturally brewed beer [bottled], **PITFIELD BREWERY**
Pitfields Original London Porter Beer [bot-
tled]

Ayingerbräu Very Strong Special Lager, D **SAMUEL SMITH**
Pils, Extra Stout, Imperial Stout, Keg Mild,
Lager, Light Ale, Natural Lager, Nut Brown
Ale, Old Brewery Bitter, Pale Ale, Prinz
Lager, Pyre Brewed Export Lager,
Sovereign Bitter, Strong Brown Ale, Strong
Golden Ale, Strong Nourishing Stout,
Strong Pale Ale, Yorkshire, 4X; [bottle]
Barley Wine, Brown Ale, Light Beer, PET
Light Mild, Premium Bitter, Premium Brown
Ale, Premium Lager Beer, Premium Pale
Ale, Premium Stout, Premium Strong
Lager, Premium Strong Stout, Strong
Lager; [bottle/can] Lager Beer, PET keg;
[keg/bottle] Bitter Stout, Kegged Premium
Bitter, Keg Mild Draught Beer; Kegged, bot-
tled, canned lager; Kegged Premium Lager,
Kegged Light Mild Draught; Low Alcohol
Lager.

Kingfisher Indian Lager [draught], Stein- **SHEPHERD NEAME**
bock Lager; Birell Low Alcohol Lager,
Pilgrims Low Alcohol Bitter

Blayneys Bitter, Blayneys Lager, Coopers **VAUX BREWERIES**
Bitter, Labatt's Lager, Norseman Lager,
Scotch Ale, Tuborg Lager

alcoholic beverages

VINCEREMOS*
Beers: Dark Star Brown Ale (UK), Flag Porter (UK); *Organic Beer:* Pinkus Lager (West Germany); *Lagers:* Pilsner Urquell (Czech); *Organic Ciders (Somerset):* Natural Dry Still Cider, Natural Sparkling Dry Cider; *Low Alcohol Lagers:* Birell (Switzerland), Clausthauler (West Germany)

H. WESTON & SONS
Packaged Ciders: Centenary Vintage (Strong Dry), Country Cider (Traditional Medium Dry), Extra Dry Cider (Original Very Dry), Perry, Special Vintage (Sweet of Dry), Supreme Cider (Extra Strong Dry), Top Line Cider (Medium Sweet), VAT 53 Cider (Medium Dry); *Traditional Draught Still Ciders:* Draught Perry (medium sweet), Farm Brand Scrumpy (dry, robust, cloudy), Old Rosie Scrumpy (very strong), Special Vintage (medium sweet, smooth, extra strong), Traditional Draught (clear, medium sweet, medium dry, dry); Marcle Orchard Low Alcohol Cider

WHITBREAD & CO
Heineken, Kaltenberg Diat Pils

YOUNG & CO
Young's London Lager, Young's Premium Lager

wines & apéritifs

DISOS
Pure Dry White Wine, Pure Dry Red Wine.

HIGHLAND WINERIES*
Blackberry Wine, Elderflower Wine, Meadowsweet Wine, Moniack Sloe Liqueur, Raspberry Wine, Silver Birch Wine

JENNINGS
Laurie Lee Fruit Wine; Eisberg Low Alcohol Wine

Martini Extra Dry, Bianco, Rosé & Rosso vermouths

MARTINI & ROSSI

Italian White: Bianco di Pontelungo, Narciso de' Poeti, Pinot Bianco del Veneto, Poggio alle Rocche, Prosecco, Verduzzo del Veneto, Vernaccia di S. Gimignano DOC; *Italian Red:* Barbera DOC Colli Tortonesi, Cabernet del Veneto, Château Chavrignac, Chianti "Bacco" DOCG, L'Olivier, Malbech del Veneto, Marzemino del Veneto, Pinot Nero del Veneto, Rosso di Vinci, Rubino di Poggio Antico; *Italian Rosé:* Rosolaccio; *Italian Dessert Wine:* Vinsanto il Cavaliere

MARK RICHARDSON TRADING*

Blackberry, Damson, Damson Gin, Elderflower, Raspberry, Sparkling Gooseberry, Spiced Elderberry wines, Sweet Plum

ROCKS COUNTRY WINES

French White (South): Côteaux Varois VDQS 1987 (Domain St Cyriaque), Gaillac AOC 1988 (Domaine de Matens), Vin de Pays de l'Aude (Domaine La Batteuse); *Bordeaux:* Bordeaux Sec AOC 1987 (Moulin de Romage), Bordeaux Supérieur Moëlleux AOC 1987 (Moulin de Romage); *Burgundy:* Bourgogne Chardonnay AOC 1987 (Chaumont), Givry AOC 1987 (Chaumont); *Champagne:* Champagne Carte d'Or (Faust), Champagne Cuvée de Réserve (Faust); *Sparkling Wines:* Blanquette de Limoux, Brut (Domaine de Batteuse); *French Rosé:* Côteaux Varois VDQS 1987 (Domaine St Cyriaque); *French Red (South):* Côteaux du Languedoc AOC 1986 (Couderc), Saint Chinian AOC 1986 (Domaine des Soulié), Vin de Pays de Côtes du Tarn (Domaine de Matens), Vin de Pays du Gard (Mas Madagascar) [5-litre glass demijohn]; *Bordeaux:* Bordeaux Supérieur AOC 1985 (Château de Prade); *Rhône:* Côtes du Rhône AOC 1987

VINATURE*

(Delacroix); *Burgundy:* Bourgogne AOC 1986 (Chaumont)

Spanish White: Mantel Nuevo DO 1987 (Alvarez y Diez)

German White: Bermersheimer Hildegardisberg QbA, Morio Muskat (Hauck)

Californian: Zinfandel 1985 (Frey)

Low-Alcohol Sparkling Wine: Pétillant de Raisin, Cuvée Réservée (Domaine de Cantalauze)

VINCEREMOS*

French Country White: Domaine de Clairac Jougla – Vin de Pays de Côtes de Thau; *Red. South:* Domaine de Clairac – Vin de pays de L'Herault, Domaine de Farlet – Vin de Pays de L'Herault 1987, Domaine de L'Attilon – Vin de pays des Bouches du Rhône 1988, Vin de Pays des Collines de La Moure 1987, Vin de Pays de L'Herault 1986 Gold Medal, Vin de Pays de L'Herault 1987; *Bordeaux:* Château Barrail des Graves St Emilion AC 1987, Château du Puy Bordeaux Supérieur AC 1979, Château La Chapelle Maillard AC 1987, Château le Barradis Bergerac Rouge AC 1986, Château Meric Graves AC 1986, Château Renaissance AC 1987; *Rhône:* Vignoble de la Jasse, AC 1986; *Burgundy:* Bourgogne Rouge Hautes Côtes de Nuits, A. Verdet AC 1986; *Beaujolais:* Château de Boisfranc, Beaujolais Supérieur AC 1988; Beaujolais Nouveau, Château de Boisfranc, AC 1989; *White. Loire:* Blanc de Blancs; Guy Bossard, Gros Plant du Pays Nantais; Gros Plant du Pays Nantais sur Lie; Guy Bossard, VDQS 1988; Muscadet de Sèvre et Maine sur Lie; Guy Bossard AC 1988; Sancerre, Christian et Nicole Dauny, AC 1988; *South:* Limoux, Domaine de Clairac, AC 1988; *Bordeaux:* Château Balluemondon Moelleux AC 1986; Château Balluemondon Sec AC 1988; Château

Canet, Entre Deux Mers, AC 1988;
Château La Chapelle Maillard Sauvignon
Sec AC 1988; Château le Barradis
Bergerac Sauvignon Sec AC; Château Le
Barradis Monbazillac AC 1986 & 1982/3;
Château Meric Graves Supérieur AC 1986;
Rhône: Châteauneuf du Pape, Pierre
André, AC 1988; *Burgundy:* Bourgogne
Blanc Chardonnay Hautes Côtes de Nuits,
A. Verdet, AC 1987; *Alsace:* Gewurz-
traminer AC 1988; Pierre Frick – Sylvaner,
AC 1986; Pinot Blanc, AC 1987; Riesling,
AC 1986; *Rosé:* Château Canet Bordeaux
Rosé, AC 1988; Château de Prade
Bordeaux Rosé, AC 1986; Domaine
Anthea, Vin de Pays de l'Aude 1988;
Champagne and Méthode Champenoise:
Clairette de Die Demi Sec, Achard-Vincent,
AC; Clairette de Die Tradition, Achard-
Vincent, AC; José Ardinat – Carte d'Or
Champagne Brut, Demi Sec & Brut Cuvée
Spéciale

Spanish Red: Biovin Valdepeñas DO
1987/8; *White:* Cava Sparkling Extra Brut,
Albet i Noya; Penedes, DO Blanco Novell,
Albet i Noya 1987/8

Italian Red: San Vito Chianti DOCG
Roberto Drighi 1987; *White:* Roberto
Drighi – San Vito Verdiglio 1987/8; San
Vito Bianco Toscano, 1987/8; San Vito Vin
Santo 1984

West German: Kerner Spatlese,
Flonheimer Geisterberg, 1986/7; Optima
Auslese, Flonheimer Klostergarten 1987;
Wurzer Kabinett, Lonsheimer Schoenberg,
1987

Apple Wine (Somerset): Cider Wine

Low-Alcohol Wine: Pétillant de Raisin,
Domaine de Matens, 1988

French White: AOC Bordeaux Sec – Moulin
de Romage '88, Bordeaux Supérieur
Moëlleux – Moulin de Romage '87, VDQS

VINTAGE ROOTS*

Gros Plant Blanc de Blancs – Bossard, AOC Anjou Sec – Domaine de Dreuillé '87/'88, AOC Limoux – Domaine de L'Ile '87, AOC Côteaux du Layon – Domaine de Dreuillé '87, AOC Muscadet de Sèvre et Maine sur lie – Bossard '88, AOC Sancerre – Dauny '87, AOC Givry – Guy Chaumont '86, AOC Châteauneuf du Pape – Pierre André '85; *French Red:* Vin de Pays du Gard – Albaric, Vin de Pays de L'Aude Cabernet – Domaine de L'Ile '87, AOC Anjou Rouge – Domaine de Dreuillé '87, AOC Bordeaux Supérieur – Château de Prade '85, AOC Beaujolais – Villages – Ducroux '87, AOC Pauillac – Château Grand Canyon, AOC Bordeaux Supérieur – Château du Puy '81/'82; *French Rosé:* AOC Rosé de Loire – Domaine de Dreuillé, AOC Cabernet d'Anjou – Domaine de Dreuillé; *Champagne & Sparkling:* Vin Mousseux – Bossard – Thuaud, AOC Clairette de Die Tradition – Achard – Vincent, AOC Anjou Brut – Domaine de Dreuillé, Champagne Carte d'Or – Faust, Champagne Cuvée de Réserve – Faust

Italian Red: Bardolino Doc Classico Superiore 1987

English White: Reichensteiner – Sedlescome '87/'88

Californian: Zinfandel – Frey '86, Cabernet Sauvignon '84

WEST HEATH WINES

French White: Ch. Chaurignac AC 1987 (Bordeaux); Ch. La Maubastit AC 1988 (Bordeaux); Ch. St Hilaire 1986 (AC Graves Supérieur); Dom du Bourdieu 1986 (AC Entre Deux Mers); Gewurztraminer 1987 (AC Vin d'Alsace); Muscat 1987 (AC Vin d'Alsace); Pinot Blanc 1986 (AC Vin d'Alsace); Puligny Montrachet 1985/6/7; *Rosé:* Ch. La Maubastit 1986 (AC Bordeaux); *Red:* Beaune 1er Cru 1985/6; Ch. Chavrignac 1986 (AC Bordeaux); Ch.

de Boisfranc (AC Beaujolais Supérieur); Ch. de Prade 1985 (AC Bordeaux Supérieur); Bourgogne Passetoutgrain AC 1985; Ch. Grand Canyon 1985; Ch. Haut Mallet 1986 (AC Bordeaux Supérieur); Ch. Jacques Blanc 1985 (AC St Emilion Grand Cru); Ch. La Maubastit 1986 (AC Bordeaux); Ch. Le Rait 1986 (AC Bordeaux Supérieur); Ch. St Hilaire 1982 (AC Graves Supérieur); Clos de La Perichère 1982 (AC Graves); Crozes Hermitage AC 1985; Hautes Côtes de Beaune AC 1985; Hautes Côtes de Nuits AC 1985; L'Enclos du Bourdieu 1987 (AC Bordeaux); L'Olivier 1987 (Vin de Pays de L'Herault); *Sparkling:* Champagne André Beaufort Brut; Champagne André Beaufort Rosé; Clairotte de Die; Le Bourdieu Brut (AC Bordeaux); Le Bourdieu Rosé (AC Bordeaux)

German: 1987 St Johannishof Muller Thurgau; 1988 Bernikasteler Schlossberg Spatlese; 1987 Lorcher Pfaffenwies Riesling; 1985 Lorcher Pfaffenwies Riesling Kabinett; 1979 Lorcher Pfaffenwies Riesling Kabinett Halbtrocken; 1987 Biebelnheimer Rosenberg Scheurebe Kabinett; 1985 Biebelheimer Pilgerstein Bacchus Spatlese; 1986 Niersteiner Rembach Riesling Kabinett; 1982 Niersteiner Kranzberg Silvaner Spatzese

Italian White: Bianco S Pietro 1987, Vino da Tavola; Soave Costeggiola 1987 DOC; *Rosé:* Chiaretto del Garda Classico 1987 DOC; *Red:* Barbera d'Alba 1986 DOC; Bardolino Classico 1987 DOC; Barolo 1984 DOCG

WHITAKER'S WINES

Alsace Tokay, Alsace Muscat, Alsace Gerwurztraminer, Mâcon, Bourgogne Rouge, Bourgogne Blanc, Pinot Noir (Alsace), Muscadet Hermine d'Or, Muscadet Silver Medal, St Hilaire Blanc, St Hilaire Rouge, Clos de la Perichère Blanc, Clos de la Perichère Rouge, Rosé d'Anjou, Rosé de Loire, Anjou Rouge, Côteaux du Layon, Haute Côte de Nuit, Beaujolais Supérieur, St Emilion Grand Cru

Elizabeth Arden is reported as having once described the cosmetics industry as "the nastiest business in the world". Whether fact or hearsay, it's a fair description, since many cosmetics and toiletries contain substances so nauseating that few thinking people would use them if the ingredients were disclosed on product labels.

Slaughterhouse by-products such as skin, tendons, ligaments and bones are boiled in water to make gelatine, used in most protein shampoos; oleic acid, comprised of various animal fats, is used in lipsticks, soaps, vanishing creams, cold creams, shaving creams, brilliantines, nail polish and perm solutions; oestrogen and progesterone, used in hormone creams, are derived from the urine of pregnant mares; crushed snails are used to add a sheen to various face creams.

The manufacture of some scents involves the use of animal fixatives and although alternatives exist, the more expensive scents are often still based upon traditional substances — such as ambergris, musk, civet or castoreum.

Ambergris is a substance coughed up by sperm whales, or taken from their stomachs after slaughter. *Musk* comes from a small pod in the abdomen of the male musk deer and although this animal is protected in its countries of origin it is still illegally hunted trapped and killed. The dried musk pod is worth more than four times its weight in gold, but infinitely more to the deer.

The African *civet* has been a source of fixatives for scents since time immemorial. The animal is kept in a small cage for several years. Every 7–10 days civet is scraped from a gland under its tail with a spatula, the whole operation requiring three attendants — the first to thrust a stick through the cage bars to secure the head, the second to open a trap door and hold the hind legs and tail, and the third to open the civet pouch with thumb and forefinger.

Castoreum, derived from glands in the groins of slaughtered (also for their fur) Canadian and Siberian beavers, provides another scent fixative, used mainly for 'masculine' fragrances.

To the above list of unethical ingredients used in the toiletries and cosmetics industry a genuinely cruelty-free stance requires the addition of less obviously objectionable ingredients — such as *lanolin*, derived from sheep's wool (including that taken from the carcases of slaughtered animals) and products such as *beeswax* and *propolis*, derived from commercial beekeeping — in which whole hives may be destroyed after honey collection to reduce the expense of keeping bees over the non-honey-producing winter months. Beeswax is made by worker bees from pairs of glands on the underside of their bodies and is used by them to build the honeycombs. Propolis is a sticky resin that bees collect with their mandibles from the resin secreted from the buds and bark of trees and shrubs and used as a filler in the hive and for embalming purposes.

In addition to its wholesale exploitation of animals for ingredients, the mainstream toiletries and cosmetics industry employs monstrously cruel methods in the testing of often trivial products. Pellets of lipstick are force-fed to laboratory animals to establish the lethal dosage, based on a 50% mortality. Shampoos and lotions are dropped into rabbits' eyes, which cannot weep and self-rinse.

The unacceptability of such barbaric testing procedures is underlined by the continuing successes within the cruelty-free movement in the development and marketing of a large and ever-expanding range of ethical alternatives.

recommended reading

Cover Up: Taking the Lid off the Cosmetics Industry, Penny Chorlton, Thorsons Grapevine, 1988

bath & shower

Bath Milks: Rosemary, Sandalwood, Thyme, Ylang Ylang — **AETHERA***

Neydharting Moor-Life Bath — **AUSTRIAN MOOR***

Drench *(unisex)* Shower Gel; *Body Shampoos & Foam Baths:* Aloe Vera, Apricot Kernel Oil, Evening Primrose, French Lavender, Green Apple, Hyacinth, Marigold Flower, Orange Blossom, Papaya, Passionflower, Tea Rose, Wild Poppy, Woodland Fern; *Creme Bath Oils:* Aloe Vera, Apricot Kernel, Green Apple, Sweetcorn; *Foaming Bath Oils:* Green Frappé, Lemon Twist, Melon Mist, Orange Froth, Passionfruit Perri, Strawberry Sensation; *Foaming Bath Oil Powders:* French Lavender, Kikui Nut, Meadow Foam, Sea Spa, Sweetcorn, Tea Rose, Wild Poppy; *Fragrance-Free range:* Foam Bath, Satin Body Wash; *Just For Men range:* Body Shampoo, Foam Bath — **BARRY M**

Marshmallow Bubbles — **BLACKMORES**

Bath Oil, Body Wash; *Bath Crystals:* Dead Sea Salt; *Bubble Baths:* Apple, Beau *(for men)*, Herbal *(for men)*, Lavender, Lemon, Lime, Orange, Strawberry, Unperfumed — **BODY & FACE PLACE**

Bath Oils: Lavender Cream, Lime, Mandarin Orange, Rose & Almond; *Bath Pearls:* Apple, Lavender, Lemon, Lilac, Peach, Rose, Strawberry, Vanilla; *Bath Salts:* Giovarni, Green Apple, Musk, Fashion, Primrose; *Bath Seeds:* Honeysuckle, Primrose, Rose, Sandalwood, White Musk; *Body Shampoos:* Herbal, Strawberry Sundae; Primrose Bubble Bath, Sandalwood Shower Soap; *Men's range:* Shampoo & Shower — **BODYLINE***

	Gel, Wash & Scrub
BODY MODE*	*Bath Oils:* Refreshing, Relaxing
BODY REFORM*	Bath Foam, Bath Oil, Shower Gel; *Bath Pearls, Bath & Shower Gel, Bubble Bath:* Chamomile & Primrose, Comfrey & Marigold, Lavender & Hawthorn, Linden & Elderflower, Orange Flower & Tansy, Rose & Thyme
BODY SHOP	Bath Oil, Bath Salts, Foaming Bath Oil, Herb Body Shampoo/Shower Gel, Orange Cream Bath Oil, Raspberry Ripple Bathing Bubbles; *Body Shampoos:* Dewberry, Strawberry; *Shower & Bath Gels:* Lavender Mint, Tea Rose, Tropics
BONITA*	*Bath Oils:* Bergamot & Peppermint, Lavender, Pine
CAMILLA HEPPER*	Caribbean Bath Foamer, Lemon Verbena Body Shampoo/Shower Gel; *Bath Oils:* Herbal Healing, Lemon Mint, Marigold; *Foam Baths:* Avocado, Orange Blossom
CARA	Almond Cream Bath; *Bath Oils:* Apricot, Jojoba, Valerian; *Foam Bath Oils:* Chamomile, Ivy, Marigold; *Men's range:* Sage Shower Gel; *Shower Gels:* Cherry, Floral, Kontiki, Strawberry
CORNUCOPIA*	*Bath Foams:* Bergamot & Ylang Ylang, Patchouli & Marjoram
COSMETICS TO GO*	Africa Wash, Aqua Sizzlers, Blackberry Bath Bomb, Champagne Bath, Grumbler, Luxury Fizzer, Red Hot Soaker, Strawberry May Fly, Turkish Bath, Vanilla Pops, Violet Nights
CREIGHTON'S	*Bath Gels:* Apple, Apricot Foaming Bath, Tangerine; *Bath Oils:* Apple, Apricot, Tan-

gerine; *Bath Seeds:* Apple, Tangerine; *Foaming Bath Seeds:* Honeysuckle, Lavender, Wild Rose

Washing Gel; *Bath oils:* Lavender, Rose, Seaweed — **CRESCENT***

Mountain Herb Shower Gel — **DAVID HILL***

Foam Baths: Coconut, Strawberry; *Shower Gels:* Coconut, Strawberry, Tropical Fruit — **DIANA B***

Body Shampoos: 6 varieties — **DOLMA***

Herbal Foam Bath, Herbal Shower Gel; *Aura range:* Foam Bath, Moisturising Bath Oil, Shower Gel — **GARLAND SKIN CARE***

Chamomile & Comfrey Old English Bath Pochette, Unperfumed Bath Oil; *Bath Delights:* Crushed Strawberry, English Apple, Oriental Ylang Ylang; *Body Shampoos:* Apple Mint & Lime, Lavender, Lemon; *Bubble Baths:* Frangipani, Lavender, Sweet Apricot, Sweet Orange & Violets; *Foaming Bath Oils:* Damask Rose, Frangipani, Rosemary, Sweet Apricot; *Shower Gels:* Lady's Mantle, Lemon Balm & Lime, Rosemary & Birch, Wild Herb — **GOODEBODIES***

Seaweed & Birch Body Shampoo — **GREEN VALLEY**

Bath Essences: Apricot & Lemon, Jasmine, Tea Rose; *Body Shampoos:* Apple & Orange, Peach & Strawberry; *Foam Baths:* Apple & Sandalwood, Pineapple & Coconut — **HONESTY***

Bath Oils & Foam Baths: Coconut, Cucumber & Glycerine, English Apple & Vitamin E, Grapefruit & Jojoba — **JAMES BODENHAM**

Bath & Shower Gel, Foaming Bath Oil — **JEAN-PIERRE SAND***

JOHNSON'S — Baby Bath

L'AROME* — Hair & Body Shampoo

LITTLE GREEN SHOP* — Tropical Fruit Foam Bath; *Body Shampoos:* Apple & Orange, Peach & Strawberry

MARTHA HILL* — Shower Gel; *Bath Oils:* Lavender, Rosemary, Sage, Seaweed & Herb

MOLTON BROWN* — Sea Moss Bath Salts, Sea Moss Shower Foam; *Bath Milks:* Deep Relaxing, Evening, Morning, Summer, Winter; *Sea Salt Crystals:* Eucalyptus, Marigold, Menthol, Mint, Rosewater

MONTAGNE JEUNESSE — *Bath Crystals:* Orange, Raspberry; *Bath Foams:* Orange Spice, Orchid, Rose; *Bath Oils:* Green Citrus, Melon, Passionfruit; *Shower Gels:* Orange Spice, Ylang Ylang

NEAL'S YARD APOTHECARY* — *Bath Oils:* Exotic, Geranium & Orange, Soothing, Stimulating; *Foaming Baths:* Arnica & Seaweed, Aromatic

NECTAR — *Bath Oils:* Apricot, Forest Mist, Honeysuckle, Island Coconut, Lemon, Morning Dew, Peach, Summer Haze, Wild Strawberry; *Bath Salts:* range of 6; *Early Care range:* Foam Bath; *Shower Gels:* Apple Acid, Apricot Foam, Country Herb, Herbal Relax, Lemon Citrus, Honeysuckle Disp, Marigold Foam, Rose & Glycerine, Strawberry, White Musk, Wild Waters

PECKSNIFF'S* — Bath Salts, Foam Bath, & Shower Gel available in a wide range of fragrances; *Aromatherapy Bath Bags:* Aching Body, Insomniacs, Morning After, Refresher

POWER HEALTH* — *Herbal Bath Sachets:* Flower Garden, Mustard Bath, Perfume Garden, Seaweed Bath, Victorian Love Bath; Comfrey, Arnica

& Witch Hazel Foam Bath; Lecithin Apricot
Bath Skin Softener

Multiherb range: Peach Beauty Bath, Vitamin E Beauty Bath

PURE PLANT

Bath Oils: Active Athletic, Anti-Stress,
Refreshing & Stimulating; *Bath Soaks:*
Active Athletic Muscle Relaxant, Calming &
Relaxing, Reviving & Refreshing; *Natural
Sea Salts:* with Coconut, w. Fresh Green
Apple, w. Grapefruit, w. Raspberry

SECRET GARDEN*

Meadowsweet & Lime Blossom Foaming
Bath Oil

TIKI

Bath Treatment Milks: Hangover Relief,
Relaxing, Reviving, Toning; *Foaming Bath
Creams:* Rosewood, Sweet Orange & Gera-
nium, X-ES

VERDE*

Bath Milks: Citrus, Lavender, Rosemary

WELEDA

Après Bain, Bain Bleu

WINSTONS*

Lace Bath Oil

YARDLEY

beauty masks

Neydharting Moor-Life Face Mask

AUSTRIAN MOOR*

Cream Face Mask

**BEAUTY WITHOUT
CRUELTY***

Herbal Clay Face Masque

BLACKMORES

Face Packs: Dead Sea Mud, Lemon & Oatmeal, Tomato

**BODY & FACE
PLACE**

Arnica, Peppermint

BODY REFORM*

BODY SHOP Aloe Peel-Off Face Mask, Camomile Face Mask

CAMILLA HEPPER* Herbal Clay, Oatmeal & Almond Oil

CARA *Facial Masks:* Almond Oil, Pineapple

CHARLES PERRY* Wheatgerm Beauty Mask

COSMETICS TO GO* *Fruit Facial Masks:* Asparagus, Cucumber, Lemon

GOODEBODIES* *Deep Cleansing Masks:* Cucumber & Parsley, Nourishing, Oatmeal & Peach; *Treatment Masks:* Dead Sea Minerals, Tropical Pineapple & Avocado

INNOXA Gentle Face Mask

JEAN-PIERRE SAND* *Advanced range:* Face Mask

MARTHA HILL* Seaweed Face Pack

MONTAGNE JEUNESSE *Face Masks:* Avocado & Pineapple, Wheatgerm & Comfrey

NECTAR *Revitalising Face Treatments:* Dry Skin, Normal Skin, Oily Skin

PIERRE CATTIER* *Masquargile:* Formula 1 *(normal and greasy)*, Formula 2 *(dry and delicate)*

POWER HEALTH* Aloe Vera Face Masque

PURE PLANT *Multiherb range:* Cucumber, Meadowmint

QUEEN* *Face Masques:* Normal/Dry, Normal/Oily

SECRET GARDEN* Anti-Stress Hydrating Gel Masque; *Clarifying Face Masques:* Clay, Marshmallow & Marigold, Sage & Fennel

deodorants etc

Deodorant	**BODY SHOP**
Watercress Deodorants	**CAMILLA HEPPER***
Deodorant; *Men's range:* Deodorant	**CARA**
No-Nonsense Deodorant	**COSMETICS TO GO***
Roll-On Deodorant	**CREIGHTON'S***
Roll-On Deodorant/Anti-Perspirant	**DAVID HILL***
Foot Shampoos: Lemon Grass & Cyprus, Peppermint & Tea Tree	**DOLMA***
Unperfumed Natural Herbal Deodorant	**GOODEBODIES***
Free & Easy Anti-Perspirant Deodorant Aerosol/Pump/Roll-On	**INNOXA**
Deodorant Body Spray	**JEAN-PIERRE SAND***
Range of deodorants	**L'AROME***
Herbal Roll-On Deodorant	**MARTHA HILL***
Roll-On: Herbal, White Musk	**NECTAR**
Odaban Anti-Perspirant Deodorant	**ODABAN**
Multiherb range: Roll-On Anti-Perspirant/Deodorant, Roll-On Anti-Perspirant/Deodorant for Men	**PURE PLANT**
Top to Toe Deodorant Powder	**QUEEN***
Deodorant with Clary Sage	**SECRET GARDEN***

toiletries & cosmetics

TRUST *Anti-odorants:* Feet, Underarm

WELEDA Citrus, Herbal

YARDLEY *Black Label, Musk Oil for Men & Pagan Man ranges:* Anti-Perspirant Deodorant, Anti-Perspirant Roll-On; *Roll-On & Sprays:* Classic Gold, Gold, Lily of the Valley, Poise, Rose, Sweet Pea, White Satin

essential oils

ALARA Range of essential oils

AROMATIQUE Wide range of essential oils

BODY & FACE PLACE Wide range of essential and blended body oils

BODY & SOUL* Wide range of essential oils

BODYLINE* Range of 17 perfume oils

BODY MODE* Range of essential oils

BODY REFORM* Wide range of essential oils

BODY SHOP Aromatherapy Range, Perfume Oils

BODYTREATS Range of bath, massage and facial oils

BONITA* Range of essential oils

BOREALIS PRODUCTS* Range of essential oils and blended massage oils

CAMILLA HEPPER* Range of essential oils

CHERISH* *Perfume Oils:* Elderflower, Lemon Verbena, Meadowsweet, Ylang Ylang

FLEUR* Range of 42 essential oils, plus ready-

toiletries & cosmetics

blended skin care, bath and massage oils

Wide range of essential oils	**GOODEBODIES***
Range of essential oils	**J. BODENHAM & CO**
Wide range of essential oils	**NEAL'S YARD APOTHECARY***
Wide range of essential oils	**NECTAR**
Wide range of essential oils	**PLENTY OF SCENTS**
Wide range of essential oils	**ROMANY***
Wide range of essential oils	**SECRET GARDEN***
Range of essential oils	**SHANTI***

eye products

Dazzle Dusts	**BARRY M**
Eye Make-Up Removing Lotion; *Kohl Pencils:* 2 colours; *Colour Option Eye Shadows:* 12 colours; *Eye Shadows:* 16 colours	**BEAUTY WITHOUT CRUELTY***
Aloe Vera Eye Gel	**BODY & FACE PLACE**
Chamomile Eye Solution, Eye Tissue Oil	**BODY & SOUL***
Eye Gel, Eye Make-Up Remover Oil	**BODYLINE***
Elderflower Eye Gel, Eye Shadows, Night Repair Eye Balm; *Kohl Pencils:* range of colours	**BODY REFORM***
Camomile Eye Make-Up Remover, Elderflower Eye Gel, Eye Make-Up Remover Oil	**BODY SHOP**

toiletries & cosmetics

CAMILLA HEPPER* Cucumber Eye Gel; *Eye Make-Up Removers:* Lotion, Oil

CARA Elderflower Eye Gel, Eye Make-Up Remover, Eye Make-Up Remover Lotion

COSMETICS TO GO* *Eye Colours:* 24 Colours; *Mascara:* 3 colours

CREIGHTON'S* Eyebright Gelée

CRESCENT* Eye Make-Up Remover, Eyelash Revitaliser

DOLMA* Eye Make-Up Remover

ENGLISH COUNTRY GARDEN* Aloe Vera Eye Gel Plus

GOODEBODIES* Angelica Night Cream, Eye Wrinkle Lotion; *Eye Gels:* Cucumber, Elderflower

HONESTY* Eye Make-Up Remover

INNOXA Creamy Powder Eye Shadows, Eye Make-Up Remover

JAMES BODENHAM Cucumber & Elderflower Eye Cream

LEICHNER Flash-Lash Mascara, Match-Stix Eye Pencils, Razzle Dazzle Loose Powder Eyeshadow; *Powder Eye Shadows:* One-Timers, Two-Timers

LITTLE GREEN SHOP* Eye Make-Up Remover

MARTHA HILL* Black Mascara, Eye Make-Up Remover, Under-Eye Cream, Under-Eye Gel; *Eye-Shadow Pots:* 6 colours

MONTAGNE JEUNESSE Eyebright Eye Gel, Eye Make-Up Remover

toiletries & cosmetics

Eye Make-Up Cleansing Oil; *Eye Gels:* Cucumber, Rose Hip, Vitamin E; *Sparkles Eye Shadow range:* 18 colours; *Trio Eye Shadow range:* 8 colours **NECTAR**

Cosmetic Eye Liners: 8 shades **PECKSNIFF'S***

Aloe Vera Eye Wrinkle Lotion **POWER HEALTH***

Epiglow Plus Eye Cream **PURE PLANT**

Eyelash Cream; *Kohl Eye Pencils:* 6 colours; *Mascara:* Black, Brown **QUEEN***

Effleurage Eye Cream 1-Minute Massage, Gentle Eye Make-Up Remover **SECRET GARDEN***

Eye Dust: entire range *(44 colours)*, *Eye liners:* entire range *(9 colours)*, *Eye Pencils:* entire range *(12 colours)*, *Eye Shadows:* entire range *(48 colours)*, *Mascara:* entire range *(11 colours)* **STARGAZER***

Multilash Mascara **YARDLEY**

face powders

Natural Dazzle *(loose powder)* **BARRY M**

Translucent Face Powders: Compressed, Loose **BEAUTY WITHOUT CRUELTY***

Finishing Touch Loose and Pressed Face Powder, Keromask Finishing Powder **INNOXA**

Loose and Pressed Face Powder, Touch & Shimmer Face Powder **LEICHNER**

Loose Powder Pots, Translucent Powder Compacts **MARTHA HILL***

toiletries & cosmetics

NECTAR	*Coloured Powders:* 4 shades
QUEEN*	13 shades
STARGAZER*	*Loose Powders:* 5 shades
ULTRA GLOW	Original Loose Face Powder
WINSTONS*	Trans. Make-Up Powder, Trans. Powder Compacts; *Compacts:* 5 shades
YARDLEY	Complexion Powder

foot care

BARRY M	Hop & Mistletoe Foot Lotion
BODY & FACE PLACE	Peppermint & Camphor Foot Oil, Soothing Foot Lotion
BONITA*	Foot Oil
CAMILLA HEPPER*	Aloe Vera Foot Lotion
CHERISH*	Foot Treatment with Peppermint
DIANA B*	Lemon & Mint Foot Lotion
DOLMA*	*Foot Shampoos:* Lemon Grass & Cyprus, Peppermint & Tea Tree
GOODEBODIES*	Clove & Sesame Foot Massage Oil, Herbal Foot Deodorant Cream, Herbal Foot Deodorant Powder with Peppermint, Refreshing Peppermint Foot Balm; *Foot Baths:* Elderberry & Sage, Jogger's Herbal
HONESTY*	Lemonmint Foot Lotion
MARTHA HILL*	Comfrey & Elder Foot Treatment Cream, Foot Balm, Seaweed & Peppermint Foot

Refresher

Foot Lotions: Cucumber & Witch Hazel, Mint & Menthol — **NECTAR**

Foot Lotions: Cucumber, Lemon, Wild Mint — **PECKSNIFF'S***

Lavinia Herbal Foot Cream — **POWER HEALTH***

Cooling & Soothing Foot Lotion — **SECRET GARDEN***

hair care

Neydharting Moor-Life Hair Tonic — **AUSTRIAN MOOR***

Hair Reviver Conditioner — **BARRY M**

Chamomile Conditioner — **BLACKMORES**

Avocado & Rosemary Hair Oil; *Conditioners:* Chamomile, Elderflower — **BODY & FACE PLACE**

Hair Massage Tonic, Scalp Massage Tonic — **BODY & SOUL***

Mellow Soap Co. Range of Conditioners: Henna, Jojoba — **BODY CARE***

Conditioners: Aloe Vera, Comfrey & Clover, Juniper; *Men's range:* Protein Conditioner — **BODYLINE***

Conditioners: Chamomile & Primrose, Comfrey & Marigold, Jojoba, Lavender & Hawthorn, Linden & Elderflower, Orange Flower & Tansy, Rose & Thyme — **BODY REFORM***

Banana Conditioner, Henna Treatment Wax, Herbal Hair Colours; *Mostly Men range:* Sedra Conditioner — **BODY SHOP**

Jojoba Conditioner — **BUAV***

toiletries & cosmetics

CAMILLA HEPPER* Avocado Treatment Wax; *Conditioners:* Herbal Protein, Natural Orange, Raspberry, Rosemary Scalp; *Natural Henna Hair Colours:* 6 shades

CARA *Conditioners:* Chamomile, Marigold, Sage & Comfrey

CHARLES PERRY* Plant Oil Conditioner

CORNUCOPIA* *Conditioners:* Jojoba & Wheat Germ, Rosemary & Lime, Thyme & Juniper

CREIGHTON'S* *Conditioners:* Lime Blossom & Birch, Orange Flower & Wheat Germ

CRIMPERS* PURE range of hypoallergenic conditioners and hair sprays for normal, dry and greasy hair

DANIEL FIELD* Essential Conditioner *(for all hair types)*, First Aid Conditioner, Plant Remoisturizing Treatment

DAVID HILL* Seaweed & Herb Conditioner, Seaweed & Herb Scalp Tonic

DIANA B* Aloe Vera Conditioner

DOLMA* Aromatherapy Hair Conditioning Oil, Nettle & Marigold Hair Lotion

ENGLISH COUNTRY GARDEN* *Conditioners:* Henna Cream, Jojoba

FRANGIPANI* Marigold Hair Conditioner

FSC Head High Hair Conditioner

GARLAND SKIN CARE* *Conditioners:* White Silk, Wild Herb

toiletries & cosmetics

Conditioners: Ginseng, Walnut & Rosemary; *Cream Conditioners:* Anti-Tangle, Avocado, Citrus Fruit Delight, Natural Vitamin E, Nettle & Rosemary *(anti-dandruff)*, Tropical Coconut; *Hair Rinses:* Chamomile, Marigold & Ginger, Protein, Walnut & Rosemary; *Hair Treatments:* Almond & Sesame Hair & Scalp Oil, Falling Hair Treatment, Natural Grey Hair Darkener, Hair Thickeners – Dark, Fair

GOODEBODIES*

Conditioners: Herbal, Sweet Orange

HONESTY*

Conditioners: Aloe Vera Jojoba, Ginseng Herbal

HOUSE OF MISTRY*

Hair Conditioner

HYMOSA

Herbal Protein Conditioner

JAMES BODENHAM

Hi-Tech *(treatment)*, Conditioner

JEAN-PIERRE SAND*

Conditioners: Aloe Vera, Herbal, Sweet Orange

LITTLE GREEN SHOP*

Hair Treatment Cream, Seaweed Hair Tonic; *Conditioners:* Seaweed & Nettle *(normal)*, Seaweed & Rosemary *(dry)*, Seaweed & Sage *(greasy)*

MARTHA HILL*

Aromatic Hair Oil, Hair Sheen For Men, Nettle Deep Shine

MOLTON BROWN*

Conditioners: Chamomile, Henna Gloss, Jojoba Oils

MONTAGNE JEUNESSE

Henna Powders: 7 shades

NECTAR

Conditioners available in a wide range of fragrances

PECKSNIFF'S*

Conditioning Balsam; *Spiritual Sky Henna Powder:* 6 colours

PLENTY OF SCENTS*

toiletries & cosmetics

POWER HEALTH*	*Conditioners:* Aloe Vera, Ginseng, Lecithin Apricot, Vitamin E Conditioner
PURE PLANT	*Conditioners:* Peach, Rosemary
SECRET GARDEN*	Rosemary De-Tangler, Scalp Oil; *PH-Balanced Conditioners:* Dry & Damaged Hair, For Extra Body, For Grease Control
SHANTI*	Hair Oil, Hair Tonic
TIKI	Country Herb Hair Conditioner
VERDE*	Coconut & Rosemary Hair Balm
WELEDA	Rosemary Creme Conditioner, Rosemary Hair Lotion

hand care

BARRY M	Hawthorn Hand Creme
BLACKMORES	Calendula Hand Creme
BODY & FACE PLACE	Barrier Hand Lotion, Rich Cocoa Butter Hand Cream
BODY REFORM*	Aloe Vera Hand Cream
BODY SHOP	Hawthorn Hand Cream
BOREALIS PRODUCTS*	Herbal Hand Cream
CAMILLA HEPPER*	Evening Primrose Hand Cream
CARA	Marigold Hand Lotion, Rich Shea Butter Hand Cream
CAURNIE	Wild Rose Hand Lotion

toiletries & cosmetics

Special Hand Treatments: Elderflower, Lemon Verbena, Meadowsweet, Ylang Ylang	**CHERISH***
Almond Oil & Cocoa Butter Hand Lotion, Bran & Sunflower Lotion, Horsetail Cuticle Cream, Olive & Almond Lotion	**GOODEBODIES***
Rich Hand Cream	**HONESTY***
Cuticle Cream	**MARTHA HILL***
Aloe Vera Hand Cream; *Hand Lotions:* Apricot & Almond, Cocoa Butter, Coconut Oil & Rose	**MONTAGNE JEUNESSE**
Hand Cream available in a wide variety of fragrances	**PECKSNIFF'S***
Multiherb Hand Lotion	**PURE PLANT**
Hand Lotion	**QUEEN***
Hand & Nail Nutrient Cream	**SECRET GARDEN***
Egyptian Chamomile Hand Soother, Italian Lemon Hand Cream	**VERDE***
Iris Hand Gel	**WELEDA**

lip products

Lip Balms: Passionfruit, Strawberry	**BODY REFORM***
Moisturising Lip Balm; *Colourings Liptints:* 01, 02, 03	**BODY SHOP**
Lip Smoothies	**CAMILLA HEPPER***
Lip Balms: Banana, Orange	**CARA**

toiletries & cosmetics

COSMETICS TO GO*	Frostbite, Mistress's Lipstick; *Lipcreams:* 7 Colours
DOLMA*	*Lipsalves with natural flavours:* 3 varieties
GOODEBODIES*	*Lip Balms:* Crushed Strawberry, Spicy Orange, Tropical Coconut
HONESTY*	Lip Service *(lip balm)*
LEICHNER	Bronzelle Lipgloss
LITTLE GREEN SHOP*	Lip Service
MARTHA HILL*	Lipgloss, Lipsalve
MONTAGNE JEUNESSE	Orange Lip Gloss Balm
NECTAR	*Lip Balms:* Blueberry Glycerine, Coconut Oil, Oil of Aloe, Rose & Glycerine, Sweet Limes
STARGAZER*	Entire range of lip glosses and lipsticks *(over 70 colours)*

nail products

BARRY M	Nail Paints
BEAUTY WITHOUT CRUELTY*	*Nail Colours:* range of 14
BODY & FACE PLACE	Hardener, Herbal Soak
BODY MODE*	Up to Scratch
BODY REFORM*	*Nail Colours:* range of shades

toiletries & cosmetics

Nail Varnish Remover	**CARA**
Nail Revitaliser	**CRESCENT***
Nail & Cuticle Oil	**DOLMA***
Protein & Mineral Nail Lotion, Sea Salt & Dill Nail-Strengthening Soak	**GOODEBODIES***
Anti Nail Bite, Base Coat, Formula N, Nail Hardener, Nail Polish Remover, Ridge Filler; *Nail Polishes:* 15 colours	**NECTAR**
Nail polishes: range of over 40 colours	**STARGAZER***
Nail Enamels: Standard Yardley and *Stayfast* ranges	**YARDLEY**

oral hygiene

Neydharting Moor-Life Mouthwash	**AUSTRIAN MOOR***
Natural Spearmint Mouthwash	**CAMILLA HEPPER***
Rowanberry Mouthwash	**CARA**
Natural Mouthwash	**GOODEBODIES***
Fennel Breath Freshener, Fennel Mouthwash, Fennel Tooth Powder	**HOLLYTREES***
Eucryl Tooth Powder	**LRC PRODUCTS**
Vicco Vajradanti Herbal Tooth Powder	**MANDALA IMPORTS***
Herbal Tooth Powder	**NATURE'S LTD***
Breath Freshener, Mouthwash	**SARAKAN**
Gargle & Mouthwash	**WELEDA**

perfumes, colognes etc

BODY & FACE PLACE
Colognes: Blossom, Frangipani, Wild Jasmine

BODYLINE*
Copycat Perfume range: Amazon, Arpino, Beau, Cleo, Giovarni, Illusion, Kiri, Narcotique, Passion, Sonata, Tempo, Zanzibar; *Men's range:* Body Splash

BODY REFORM*
Range of 14 *parfums de toilette* and three *colognes pour hommes*

BONITA*
Floral Waters: Orange Flower, Rose, Witch Hazel

CAMILLA HEPPER*
Teaza Splash Cologne

CHANDORÉ*
All perfumes

COSMETICS TO GO*
Perfumes: Ginger, Pas de Musque, Salarum

DAVID HILL*
Cologne

DOLMA*
Perfumes: 6 varieties

ENGLISH LAKES*
Wide range of perfumes and *eaux de toilette*

GARLAND SKIN CARE*
All perfumes and fragrances

GOODEBODIES*
Wide range of perfume oils

HONESTY*
Rosewater; *Perfume Pots:* Flower Pot, Honey Pot, Tea Pot

JAMES BODENHAM
Classic range: Cologne

JEAN-PIERRE SAND*
Wide range of *eaux de parfum*

Wide range of natural perfumes, toilet waters etc. Bespoke service available.

KITTYWAKE*

Range of colognes and *eaux de parfum*

L'AROME*

Fragrances: No.1, No.2, No.3, No.4

MARTHA HILL*

Toilet Waters: Blue Hyacinth, Dianthus, Jasmine, Winter Sweet

MOLTON BROWN*

Solid Perfumes: Honeysuckle, Jasmine

OXFAM*

Wide range of perfumes, toilet waters etc. Bespoke service available.

PECKSNIFF'S*

Spiritual Sky Eau de Toilette: 18 fragrances

PLENTY OF SCENTS

Cherisse, Moonflower, Sophistica

PURE PLANT

Custom-Blend Cologne *(for men)*; *Eaux de toilette and Perfumes:* Active Blend, Classic Blend, Evening Blend

SECRET GARDEN*

Perfume Pot *(rose-scented)*

TRAIDCRAFT*

YARDLEY

Body Sprays: April Violets, Lavender, Lavender & Rosemary, Lavender & Thyme, Lily of the Valley, Musk Oil for Women, Pagan for Women, Roses, Sweet Pea; *Cologne Sprays:* Black Velvet, Chique, ESP, Flair, Freesia, Lace, Lavender, Lily of the Valley, Musk Oil for Women, Pagan for Women, Petunia, Pink Lace, Pure Silk, Roses, Sweet Pea, White Satin; *Liquid Colognes:* Black Velvet, Lace, Pink Lace, Pure Silk, White Satin; *Parfums de Toilette:* Black Velvet, Chique; *Perfumes:* Chique, Musk Oil for Women, Pagan for Women; *Perfume Sprays:* Black Velvet, Lace, Pink Lace, Pure Silk, White Satin

toiletries & cosmetics

shampoos

AUSTRIAN MOOR*   Neydharting Moor-Life Shampoo

BARRY M   Aloe Vera Coconut Ice, Camomile, Green Apple, Henna, Jojoba Conditioning, Just For Men Ginseng, Just Herbal, Marigold & Birch, Oil of Orchid, Orange Spice & Arnica, Rosemary & Willow, Sage & Dandelion, Seaweed & Nettle, Tofu & Soya Protein

BLACKMORES   Marshmallow, Wild Nettle

BODY & FACE PLACE   Blue Peppermint, Chamomile, Citrus, Elderflower, Jojoba with Rosemary, Red Apple; *Frequent Wash:* Henna & Ginger, Soapwort

BODY & SOUL*   Chamomile & Avocado, Jojoba & Avocado, Pure *(unperfumed)*, Rosemary & Avocado

BODY CARE*   *Mellow Soap Co. Range of Shampoos:* Henna, Jojoba

BODYLINE*   Aloe Vera, Camomile, Deep Ocean Mud, Herb Cocktail Rejuvenating, Litchen Anti-Dandruff, Nettle & Lime Flowers, Peppermint, Rosemary, White Henna Cream, Wild Cherry, Willow & Birch Conditioning

BODY REFORM*   *Daily-Use Shampoos:* Chamomile & Primrose, Comfrey & Marigold, Lavender & Hawthorn, Linden & Elderflower, Orange Flower & Tansy, Rose & Thyme; *Non-Emulsified Shampoos:* Aloe Vera, Peppermint, Rosemary

BODY SHOP   Camomile Powder Shampoo, Camomile Shampoo, Coconut Oil Shampoo, Frequent Wash Grapefruit Shampoo, Henna Cream Shampoo, Jojoba Oil Conditioning Shampoo, Seaweed & Birch Shampoo; *Mostly Men range:* Rhassoul Mud Shampoo

Henna, Jojoba **BUAV***

Camomile, Coconut Oil, Herbal Healing, Jojoba Oil, Lavender & Sesame Oil, Natural Orange, Rosemary, Ti-Tree & Thyme, Watercress **CAMILLA HEPPER***

Baby, Chamomile, Frequency Wash, Marigold, Mountain Arnica, Rosemary, Sage & Comfrey, Treatment; *Men's range:* Conditioning Shampoo, Medicated Shampoo **CARA**

Avocado, Pure **CAURNIE**

Coconut Oil **CHARLES PERRY***

Lavender & Nettle *(for frequent use)*, Rosemary & Lime *(normal hair)*, Tea Tree & Lemon *(dandruff treatment)*, Thyme & Juniper *(greasy hair)*, Jojoba & Wheatgerm *(damaged hair)*; Chamomile & Yarrow, Vitamin E & Wheatgerm **CORNUCOPIA***

Khufu, King Coconut, Sea-Level Seaweed Shampoo, Serpentine; *Shampoo Bars:* Inasia Coconut, Inasia Dead Sea Salt **COSMETICS TO GO***

Apricot, Chamomile & Wheat Germ, Lime Blossom & Rosemary, Orange Flower & Birch, Watercress & Almond, Yarrow & Wild Nettle; *Conditioning Shampoos:* Apple, Comfrey, Tangerine **CREIGHTON'S***

Sage **CRESCENT***

PURE range of hypoallergenic shampoos for normal, dry and greasy hair **CRIMPERS***

Frequent Wash Scalp Therapy, Medicated **DANIEL FIELD***

(oily hair), Remoisturizing (dry hair), Revitalising (normal hair), Spring Water Frequent Wash

DAVID HILL*   Green Herbal, Protein, Seaweed & Herb

DIANA B*   Aloe Vera (normal), Avocado (frequent use), Jojoba (dry hair), Lemon & Mint (greasy hair), Rosemary & Nettle (medicated)

DOLMA*   Nettle & Pectin Shampoos (with essential oils): 5 varieties

ENGLISH COUNTRY GARDEN*   Camomile, Rosemary

FAITH   Aloe Vera, Jojoba, Rosemary, Seaweed

FAMILY CARE   Natural Plant & Fruit Extract: Cucumber, Jojoba, Sandalwood

FRANGIPANI*   Apple Mint, Henna, Jojoba, Marigold, Rosemary & Nettle, Seaweed

FSC   Head High Hair Shampoo

GARLAND SKIN CARE*   Jojoba Oil, Mild Shampoo, Wild Herb Conditioning

GOODEBODIES*   After Sun & Sea Hair Conditioning, Chamomile & Lemon, Country Apple, Daily, Elderflower Conditioning, Ginseng, Kelp & Jaborandi Hair & Scalp, Lime Blossom & Almond, Marigold & Ginger, Natural Jojoba Oil, Natural Vitamin E, Nettle & Rosemary Anti-Dandruff, Tropical Coconut

GREEN VALLEY   Chamomile, Rosemary

HAAR SANA*   Millet Shampoo

HONESTY*   Apple, Chamomile & Orange, Herbal, Nettle, Peach & Coconut

Aloe Vera Jojoba, Ginseng Herbal	**HOUSE OF MISTRY***
Anti-Dandruff, Dry Hair, Family, Greasy	**HYMOSA**
Camomile, Henna Conditioning, Rosemary & Glycerine	**JAMES BODENHAM**
Gentle Anti-Dandruff, Ultra-Sensitive	**JEAN-PIERRE SAND***
Country Garden, Green Apple, Green Clover, Herbal, Orange Blossom, Peach Blossom, Rose, Wild Flower	**LITTLE GREEN SHOP***
Seaweed & Nettle *(normal)*, Seaweed & Rosemary *(dry)*, Seaweed & Sage *(greasy)*	**MARTHA HILL***
Camomile, Daily, Extra Mild Shampoo For Men, Rosemary	**MOLTON BROWN***
Chamomile, Henna Gloss, Seaweed	**MONTAGNE JEUNESSE**
Calendula, Chamomile & Orange, Coconut & Jojoba, Henna, Nettle & Sage, Rosemary & Thyme, Seaweed	**NEAL'S YARD APOTHECARY***
Aloe Vera, Camomile, Coconut, Dantex, Green Apple, Jojoba, Lemon Citrus, Rosemary; *Early Care range:* Shampoo; *Geisha range:* Dandruff, Dry, Normal, Oily	**NECTAR**
Scented Shampoos available in a wide variety of fragrances; *Treatment Shampoos:* Avocado *(frequent wash)*, Baby, Chamomile, Coconut, Henna *(dry hair)*, Lime *(greasy)*, Rosemary & Nettle *(medicated)*	**PECKSNIFF'S***
Moussargile: Dry Hair Formula, Greasy Hair Formula	**PIERRE CATTIER***

toiletries & cosmetics

POWER HEALTH*
Aloe Vera, Apple, Chamomile, Honeysuckle, Lavender, Lecithin Apricot, Peach, Rose, Vitamin E; *(fancy bottles)* Apple Dash, Apricot Velvet, Banana Split, Raspberry Sundae, Royal Victoria, Strawberry Fields; *Nature Knows Best range:* Cucumber, Ginseng, Rosemary, Seaweed, Wheatgerm & Nettle

PURE PLANT
Multiherb range: Medicated, Peach Conditioning Cream, Rosemary

QUEEN*
Shampoo

SECRET GARDEN*
Anti-Dandruff, City Protection, For Dry Damaged Hair, For Extra Body, For Frequent Use, For Grease Control; *Special Shine range:* For Blonde & Light Brown Hair, For Dark Hair, For Red & Auburn Hair

SHANTI*
Herbal

SIMONE CHANTEL
Herbal Gloss

TIKI
Camomile, Marigold, Nettle, Rosemary

WELEDA
Calendula, Lemon & Melissa, Rosemary, Rosemary & Chamomile

shaving products

AUSTRIAN MOOR*
Neydharting Moor-Life Aftershave

BODY & FACE PLACE
Herbal Aftershave

BODYLINE*
Aftershave Balm; *Aftershaves:* Larwood, Titus, Zardos

BODY REFORM*
Aftershave Cream

Mostly Men range: After Shaves, Face Protector, Shaving Creams	**BODY SHOP**
Birch Shaving Cream, Panther Aftershave	**CAMILLA HEPPER***
Aftershave Balm, Shaving Cream	**CARA**
Soothing Aftershave Balm	**CHERISH***
Carter's Shaving Cream	**COSMETICS TO GO***
Aftershave Gel, Aftershave Moisturiser & Skin Shield, Cleansing & Shaving Cream	**DAVID HILL***
Men's Challenge range of Aftershave, Cologne & Pre-Electric: 5-Star, Flying 15, Summit	**ENGLISH LAKES***
Aftershaves: Prohibition, Razzel	**HONESTY***
Classic range: Aftershave Lotion, Aftershave Soothing Balm	**JAMES BODENHAM**
Men's Fragrances: Aftershave Balm, Aftershave Splash-On, Concentrated Cologne, Sports Cologne	**JEAN-PIERRE SAND***
Range of aftershaves	**L'AROME***
Aftershaves: Prohibition, Razzle	**LITTLE GREEN SHOP***
Aftershave Balms & Aftershave Oils/Lotions: Aramis, Drakkar Noir, French Line, Lacoste, Paco Rabane, Polo; *Shaving Soaps/Creams:* Kouros, Lavender, Sandalwood	**NECTAR**
Wide range of aftershaves. Bespoke service available.	**PECKSNIFF'S***
Aftershave Tonic, Custom-Blend Aftersh-	**SECRET GARDEN***

ave, Shaving Cream Soap with Vitamin E, Soothing & Healing Aftershave Bar

SHANTI* Shaving Lotion

YARDLEY Gold Aftershave Spray; *Aftershaves:* Classic Gold, Gold, Musk Oil for Men, Pagan Man; *Pre-Electric:* Black Label, Classic Gold, Gold

skin care

AUSTRIAN MOOR* *Neydharting Moor-Life range:* Cleansing/Toning Lotion, Massage Oil, Salve/Body Cream, Skin Cream/Face Cream

BACK TO NATURE* Lemon Balm Lotion; *Creams:* Avocado Night, Marigold, Meadowsweet, Rose Petal; *Skin Tonics:* Combination, Dry, Oily

BARRY M After-Massage Toner, Massage Gel, Massage Milk, Papaya Gel Moisturising Creme, Sarsaparilla Sluffer *(facial scrub)*, Sweet Fennel Cleansing Milk; *Cleansing Lotions:* Aloe Vera, Avocado & Cucumber, Oatmeal & Lemon, Papaya, Passionflower; *Facial Toners:* Aloe Vera, Marigold & Mallow, Papaya, Passionflower, Rosewater & Witch Hazel, Sage, Comfrey & Cucumber, Sweet Fennel; *Fragrance-Free Collection:* Cleansing Lotion, Hand & Body Lotion, Facial Toner; *Hand & Body Lotions:* Aloe Vera, Apricot Kernel Oil, Evening Primrose, French Lavender, Green Apple, Hyacinth, Marigold Flower, Orange Blossom, Papaya, Passionflower, Tea Rose, Wild Poppy, Woodland Fern; *Just For Men range:* Body Balm, Facial Moisturising Gel

BEAUTY WITHOUT CRUELTY* Avocado Moisturiser, Facial Cleansing Bar, Rose Petal Skin Freshener, Scrub Cream,

Sunflower & Wheat Cream; *Flowers of Lilac range:* Cleansing Cream, Hand Lotion

Almond Cleansing Creme, Avocado Night Creme, Cucumber Cleanser, Evening Primrose Body Lotion, Marshmallow Moisturiser, Thyme Lotion, White Ivy Body Scrub, Witch Hazel Toner,

BLACKMORES

Aloe Vera Moisture Plus, Cocoa Butter Body Lotion, Elderflower Cleansing Cream, Facial Sauna, Oatmeal Facial Rub; *Cleansing Milks:* Cocoa Butter, Elderflower, Jasmine; *Moisturisers:* Elderflower, Marshmallow; *Skin Toners:* Chamomile, Cucumber, Elderflower & Orange, Marigold & Lavender

BODY & FACE PLACE

Comfrey & Vitamin E Cream

BODY & SOUL*

Apricot Neck Cream, Avocado & Almond Moisture Cream, Lemon & Oatmeal Facial Scrub, Marigold Moisture Cream, Oatmeal Facial Lather, Vitamin A Anti-Wrinkle Cream; *Lotions:* Aloe Vera Lotion, Body Massage Oil, Carrot Cleaning & Nourishing Milk, Great Grandmother's Facial Wash; *Toners:* Elderflower Water, Elizabethan Skin Tonic, Orange Flower Water

BODYLINE*

Facial Mist; *Body Oils:* Moisturising, Sports

BODY MODE*

Aloe Vera Day Cream, Aloe Vera Moisturising Lotion, Avocado Night Nourishing Cream, Decolleté Cream, Hand & Body Lotion, Peppermint Day Cream, Roll-On Wrinkle Care, Rosemary Cleansing Milk, St John's Wort Day Cream, Walnut Facial Scrub, Wheatgerm Night Nourishing Cream; *Cleansers, Cocoa Butter Moisturisers, Hand & Body Lotions, Rich Moisturising Creams, Soothing Day Creams, Vitamin E Creams:* Chamomile & Primrose, Com-

BODY REFORM*

frey & Marigold, Lavender & Hawthorn, Linden & Elderflower, Orange Flower & Tansy, Rose & Thyme; *Toner Lotions*: Chamomile, Orange, Peppermint

BODY SHOP

Aloe Body Spray, Aloe Gel, Aloe Lotion, Aloe Vera Moisture Cream, Apricot Kernel Oil, Body Massage Oil, Body Sunblock, Carrot Facial Oil, Cellulite Massage Oil, Cocoa Butter Hand & Body Lotion, Dewberry 5-Oils Lotion, Elderflower Water, Evening Primrose Oil, Glycerine & Rosewater Lotion with Vitamin E, Glycerine & Oat Facial Lather, Japanese Washing Grains, Jojoba Oil, Neck Gel, Orange Flower Water, Orchid Oil Cleansing Milk, Passion Fruit Cleansing Gel, Rice Bran Body Scrub, Rich Massage Lotion, Sage & Comfrey Open Pore Cream, Sweet Almond Oil, White Grape Skin Tonic

BONITA*

Breast Firming Oil, Cucumber Cleansing Lotion; *Moisturizers:* Cocoa Butter, Marshmallow, Rosewater, Wheatgerm; *Toners:* Orange Blossom, Rosewater

BOREALIS PRODUCTS*

AntiWrinkle Oil, Avocado & Yarrow Face Cream, Cocoa Butter & Rosewater Moisturising Lotion, Cocoa Butter Cleanser, Herbal Toner with Cider Vinegar, Lavender & Seaweed Moisturising Lotion, Orange Flower Water

BUAV*

Calendula Moisturiser

CAMILLA HEPPER*

Azufre Cleanser, Camilla's Cleansing Cream, Exfoliating Tropical Skin Polisher, Facial Wash Cream, Lettuce Moisture Whip, Marsa-Med Cleansing Bar, Mint & Olive Stone Scrub, Rich Skin Food, T-Zone Balancing Freshener, T-Zone Foaming Cleanser; *Cleansing Milks:* Lemon Balm, Meadowsweet; *Creams:* Avocado Moisture, Azufre, Herbal, Regenerative, T-Zone Moisturising Control, Wheatgerm & Marigold Moisture; *Flower Waters:* Orange, Rose; *Lotions:* Azufre, Jojoba Oil Moisture, Orange Blossom & Cocoa Butter Body; *Skin Demands For Men range:* Face Protection, Face Wash; *Skin Toners:* Elderflower, Yarrow

CARA

Avocado Moisture Cream, Camphor Lotion, Cucumber Cleansing Milk, Cucumber Face Tonic, Elderflower Complex, Elderflower Freshener, Evening Primrose Neck Cream, Herbal Cleansing Milk, Herbal Cream, Lemon Facial Scrub, Jojoba Lotion, Lime Blossom Cleansing Cream, Medicated Cream, Pineapple Facial Wash, Sage & Yarrow Skin Tonic, Vitamin E Cream, Vitamin E Oil, Witch Hazel Toner; *Fragrance-Free range:* Evening Primrose Night Cream, Linden Flower Moisturiser, Marshmallow Cleansing Lotion, Orchid Day Cream; *Men's range:* Lemon Facial Scrub, Protein Moisturiser

CHARLES PERRY*

Indian Elm Foundation, Sunflower Tissue Oil, Wheatgerm Beauty Balm; *Deep Cleansers:* Almond, Lemon

CHERISH*

Carrot Facial Oil, Sweet Almond Oil, Wheatgerm Oil; *Body Oils:* Avocado & Ylang Ylang, Carotene & Elderflower, Marigold & Lemon Verbena, Wheatgerm & Meadowsweet; *Cleansers:* Carotene & Elderflower Cream, Orange & Almond Beauty Grains, Wheatgerm & Lemon Verbena Cream; *Floral Waters/Toners:* Chamomile, Elderflower, Orange Flower; *Moisturizers:* Avocado & Ylang Ylang, Carotene Anti-Wrinkle Fragrance Free, Carotene Anti-Wrinkle with Elderflower, Marigold & Lemon Verbena, Wheatgerm & Meadowsweet

CORNUCOPIA*

Cleansing Cream, Exfoliating Scrub, Face

Shampoo, Oil-Free Cleanser; *Moisturizing Face Creams:* Bergamot & Naiouli, Cypress & Chamomile, Geranium & Lime, Lavender & Rose Geranium

COSMETICS TO GO* Alacalufa, Cold Comfort, Dry Face Moisturiser, Hand & Body Moisturiser, Massage Oil, Miriam *(soapless facial cleansing bar)*, Pagoda Tree Cleanser, Pagoda Tree Moisturiser, Vanishing Cream; *Fruit Facial Cleansers:* Avocado, Papaya

CREIGHTON'S* Apricot Facial Gel, Apricot Facial Oil, Apricot Scrub Mask, Evening Primrose Facial Wash, Sage & Comfrey Deep Cleansing Cream; *Cleansing Lotions:* Apricot, Evening Primrose, with Linden Flowers; *Hand & Body Lotions:* Apricot, Evening Primrose, May Blossom & Comfrey; *Moisturising Lotions:* Apricot, Evening Primrose, Comfrey & Vitamin E; *Toning Lotions:* Apricot, Evening Primrose, Rosemary

CRESCENT* Almond Massage Oil, Cucumber & Witch Hazel Skin Freshener, Lemon & Olive Cleansing Lotion, Rose Skin Tonic, Sunflower & Orange Moisturising Cream

DAVID HILL* Multi-purpose Cream, Outdoor Sports Protection Cream, Outdoor Sports Protection Gel

DOLMA* *Aromatherapy Facial Oils:* 7 varieties; *Moisturizing Creams:* 3 varieties; *Toners:* Astringent, Gentle

ENGLISH COUNTRY GARDEN* *Aloe Vera range:* Aloe Cleanser, Apple Blossom Hand & Body Lotion, Moisture Lotion, Skin Food; *Avocado, Wheat Germ & Vitamin E range:* Moisture Cream, Skin Food; *Skin Toners:* English Rose, Orange Flower Water

Almond Scrub, Body Oil, Jojoba Moisturising Lotion, Rosewater Toning Lotion **FAITH**

Body Oil, Cleansing Mousse, Cucumber & Witch Hazel Tonic, Granular Facial Scrub, Orange Oil Tonic, Pure Rosewater, Sage & Comfrey Complexion Gel **FRANGIPANI***

Oil of Orchid range: Day Moisture Base, Gentle Cleansing Lotion, Gentle Freshener, Nourishing Night Treatment **FSC**

Almond & Wheat Germ Hand & Body Lotion, Avocado Active Moisturiser, Elderflower & Marigold Gentle Toner, Jojoba Cleansing Lotion, Tangerine Cream Wash, Wild Herb Toner; *Aura range:* Body Lotion **GARLAND SKIN CARE***

Aloe Gel, Azuki Beans Washing Grains; *Creams:* Banana & Apricot Wrinkle, Cocoa Butter & Almond Oil Delicate Facial, Horsetail & Lemon Pore, Lemon & Almond Wrinkle, Marigold Threaded Vein, Neck & Throat, Stretch Mark; *Exfoliating Cleansers:* Apricot & Avocado, Peach and Azuki Bean, Peppermint & Ground Walnut Shell; *Facial Cleansers:* Comfrey & Jojoba, Cocoa Butter & Sunflower, Cucumber & Yarrow, Lemon & Oatmeal, Olive & Avocado, Rose & Almond Oil; *Facial Toners:* Applemint & Lime, Cider & Witch Hazel, Old-Fashioned Flower Waters – Elderflower, Lavender, Rose; *Facial Washes:* Beech & Almond Oil, Tropical Pineapple; *Ginseng range:* Body Moisturising Lotion, Cleanser, Facial Toner, Moisturiser; *Leg Care range:* Bergamot Leg-Shaving Oil, Peppermint Leg Gel; *Lotions:* Aloe, Delicate Herbal Skin, English Rose & Cucumber Moisturising Body; *Make-Up Removers:* Applemint & Lime, Natural with Herbs; *Moisturisers:* Aloe Vera, Avocado, Dead Sea Mineral, Evening **GOODEBODIES***

Primrose, Jojoba, Rich Carrot; *Over-30s range:* Day Cream, Cleanser, Moisturiser, Night Cream; *Vitamin E range:* Body Moisturising Lotion, Cleanser, Moisturiser, Toner

GREEN VALLEY

Rosewood Hand & Body Lotion; *Cleansers:* Comfrey & Yarrow, Cucumber, Lemon Balm; Facial Scrub, Gentle Washing Cream; *Moisture Creams:* Aloe Vera & Jojoba, Comfrey & Chamomile, Lady's Mantle; *Skin Tonics:* Comfrey, Orange Flower, Rosewater, Yarrow & Lovage

HONESTY*

Orange Hand & Body Lotion; *Cleansing Lotions & Toners:* Chamomile & Orange Flower, Marigold & Elderflower; *Herbal Face Saunas:* Dry Skin, Oily Skin; *Moisturizers:* Avocado & Wheat Germ Nourishing Cream, Cocoa Butter Moisturizing Lotion, Moisturizing Cream

HOUSE OF MISTRY*

Aloe Vera Cocoa Butter Moisturising Cream, Evening Primrose Oil, Ginseng Cleanser & Toner, Ginseng Herbal Scrub, Ginseng Moisturising Cream with Vitamin E, Ginseng Night Cream, Vitamin E Cream, Vitamin E Oil

HYMOSA

Cleansing Milk, Hand & Body Lotion, Moisturising Lotion, Skin Freshener, Vitamin E Creme

INNOXA

71 Barrier Cream, Alcohol-Free Toner, Mousse Foundation, On & Off Depilatory Cream; *(for sensitive/normal skin)* Conditioning Toner, Cream Moisturiser, Liquid Cleanser; *(for sensitive/oily skin)* Astringent Toner, Facial Scrub, Oil-Free Moisturiser, Rinse-Away Cleanser; *The 41 range (for very oily/blemished skin):* Astringent Toner, Protective Moisturising Lotion, Skin Shampoo, Solution; *(all skin types)*

Active-Life Moisturiser, Moisture Oil of Amalene

Herbal Hand & Body Lotion, Wheatgerm & Aloe Vera Night Cream; *Cleansing Milks:* Lime Blossom, Marigold; *Massage Oils:* Avocado & Vitamin E, Jojoba & Lavender; *Moisture Creams:* Avocado & Vitamin E, Camomile; *Toning Lotions:* Cucumber, Elderflower, Rosewater

JAMES BODENHAM

Body Lotion, Perfumed Body Oil; Liposand *(anti-ageing complex)*; *Advanced range:* Anti-Wrinkle Cream, Cleansing Milk, Day Cream, Exfoliator, Night Cream, Toner

JEAN-PIERRE SAND*

Baby Oil

JOHNSON'S

Avocado & Wheatgerm Nourishing Cream, Cocoa Butter Moisturising Lotion, Cocoa Butter Hand & Body Lotion; *Body Oils:* Frangipani & Ylang Ylang, Jasmin & Tea Rose, Sandalwood & Orange; *Cleansers & Toners:* Camomile & Orange, Marigold & Elder

LITTLE GREEN SHOP*

Vicco Turmeric Skin Cream

MANDALA IMPORTS*

Banana Body Lotion, Body Lotion, Cleansing Milk, Day Cream, Evening Primrose Multi-Purpose Cream, Hydro Cream, Massage Cream, Night Cream, Seaweed & Orange Body Oil, Skin Tonic, Spray-On Skin Refresher, Toning Gel

MARTHA HILL*

Clarify, Cleanse, Deep Cleanse Kit – Type 1, Type 2, Moisture Retainer, Tone 1, Tone 2, Wash

MOLTON BROWN*

Aloe Vera Anti-Wrinkle Night Cream, Aloe Vera Body Moisturising Gel, Apricot Astrin-

MONTAGNE JEUNESSE

gent Lotion, Apricot Body Moisturiser, Black Grape Body Oil, Comfrey Herbal Face Lotion, Cucumber Moisturising Cream, Evening Primrose Body Moisturiser, Melon Anti-Wrinkle Cream, Peach & Almond Vitamin E Night Cream, White Grape Massage Oil; *Cleansing Milks:* Avocado, Cucumber; *Skin Toners:* Cucumber, Witch Hazel

NEAL'S YARD APOTHECARY*

Cleansers: Calendula, Chamomile, Sage & Elderflower; *Moisturisers:* Frankincense & Myrrh Revitalising Cream, Rosewater & Glycerine, Sandalwood & Jasmine; *Skin Toners:* Chamomile Flower Water, Flower Freshener, Lavender Water, Orange Flower Water, Rosewater, Witch Hazel

NECTAR

Neck Gel; *Cleansing Lotions & Moisture Lotions:* Aloe Vera, Avocado, Lemon & Camomile, Rose & Glycerine, Wheatgerm; *Depilatory Treatment:* Taky Creme; *Early Care range:* Baby Lotion, Baby Oil, Nappy Cream; *Facial Scrubs:* Azuki Grains, Dead Sea Mud, King Island Clay, Lemon & Oatmeal, Pineapple & Avocado Stone, Sandalwood & Olive Stone; *Hand & Body Lotions:* Aloe Vera, Cocoa Butter, Jojoba, White Musk; *Moisture Cremes:* Aloe Vera Day, Aloe Vera Night, Aloe Vera Rich, Avocado, Carrot Mousse, Jojoba Oil, Moisture Plus, Wheatgerm Anti-Wrinkle; *Moisturising Body Treatment:* Aramis, Drakkar Noir, French Line, Lacoste, Paco Rabane, Polo; *Toning Tonics:* Aloe Vera, Lemon & Camomile, Rose & Glycerine, Wheatgerm

PECKSNIFF'S *

Cleansing Milks, Moisturising Milks, Night Creams & Toning Skin Tonics: Arnica & Marigold, Burdock & Orange Flower, Elderflower & Lime, Mountain Grape, Rose & Aloe Vera

PIERRE CATTIER*

Argicreme Night Cream, Lactargile Make-

Up Remover, Tonique Lotion; *Argicreme Day Cream Formulas:* Dry, Greasy, Normal

Skin Clear Lotion

PLENTY OF SCENTS

Lecithin Apricot Super Moisturizing Cream, Pure Vegetable Glycerine; *Aloe Vera range:* Body Lotion, Day Cream, Healing Gel, Night Cream, Skin Cleanser, Skin Toner; *Vitamin E range:* Cream, Natural Oil, Skin Conditioner;

POWER HEALTH*

Aloe Vera Moisturising Cream, Cream of Orchids, Cucumber Moisture Base, Peaches & Cream Beauty Care with Vitamin E, Peach Foundation; *Epiglow range:* Beauty Cream, Neck Firming Cream, Regenerative Cream for Night & Day, Special Nourishing Night Cream; *Epiglow Hypoallergenics range:* Cleansing Lotion, Day Moisture Base, Moisturising Lotion, Night Cream; *Multiherb range:* Aloe Vera Moisturising Lotion, Astringent, Cleansing Lotion, Cucumber Moisturising Lotion, Deep Moisture, Orange Flower Skin Toner, Peach Facial Scrub, Super-Cleanse, Witch Hazel Cream; *Oil of Orchid range:* Day Moisture Base, Gentle Cleansing Lotion, Gentle Freshener, Nourishing Night Treatment

PURE PLANT

Astringent Lotion, Medicated Cleansing Lotion, Moisturiser, Muscle Oil, Non-Alcoholic Toning Lotion, Skin Freshener

QUEEN*

Aloe Vera & Walnut Flake Body Scrub, Antiseptic Treatment Cream, Crushed Almond Face Scrub, Double-Action Facial Grains, Facial Protection Cream, Facial Protection Emulsion, Moisturising Emulsion For Men, Rose-Geranium Neck Gel, White Grape & Marigold Toner, Wild Thyme & Violet Astringent; *Body Massage Oils & Lotions:* Active Athletic, Anti-Stress, Refreshing & Stimu-

SECRET GARDEN*

lating; *Cleansers:* Mandarin & Oat, Milky Liquid; *Moisturising Lotions & Nourishing Creams:* Aloe Vera & Marshmallow, Wheatgerm & Yarrow Oil, Wild Lettuce & Hamamelis; *Nutrient Skin Creams & Nutrient Skin Tonics:* Comb/Normal, Comb/Oily, Dry/Sensitive; *Variations range:* Personalised Massage Oil, Personalised Skin Cream, Complex Cream, Massage Oil

TIKI

Marigold Cream, Vitamin E High-Potency Oil, Vitamin E Moisturiser; *Cleansers, Moisturisers & Toners:* Camomile, Cucumber & Lime Blossom, Witch Hazel

VERDE*

Grapefruit Mousse Moisturiser; *Body Milks:* Bergamot & Lavender, Sandalwood & Rose, Sweet Orange & Geranium; *Body Performance Oils:* Relaxing, Reviving, Toning; *Cleansing Milks:* Lavender, Palma Rosa; *Facial Treatment Oils:* Calendula & Evening Primrose, Orange Blossom & Rose; *Toning Lotions:* Elderflower & Bergamot, Orange Blossom & Rose

WELEDA

Citrus Body Toner, Silver Birch Massage Oil; *Iris Skin Care range:* Cleansing Milk, Facial Oil, Moisturising Lotion

WINSTONS*

Beauty Milk, Night Nourishing Cream, Skin Tonic; *Day Creams:* Dry, Regular

YARDLEY

Beauty Magic Skin Freshener; *Splash-On Lotions:* Classic Gold, Gold, Musk Oil for Men

skin make-up

BODY REFORM*   *Blushers:* range of shades

BODY SHOP   *Colourings range:* Cream Blush, Translucent Bronzer

Gigaku Foundation 1, Gigaku Foundation 2, Liquid Stockings *(make-up for legs)*; *Blushers:* 7 shades	**COSMETICS TO GO***
Soft Powder Blusher; *41 Range:* Foundation *(all shades)*	**INNOXA**
Make-Up Compacts	**JEAN-PIERRE SAND***
Bronzelle Fluid Tint, Cheek Tricks Blushers	**LEICHNER**
Cover-Up Cream; *Sun Barrier Foundation:* 4 shades	**MARTHA HILL***
Duo Blushers: 4 shades	**NECTAR**
Tinted Foundation Creams: 4 shades	**QUEEN***
Liquid Foundation: 5 shades	**STARGAZER***
Cream Up: Dark, Light; *Liquid Make-Up:* 5 shades; *Trans. Cream Make-Up:* Nos. 2, 4,6	**WINSTONS***

soaps

Sandalwood Beauty Soap	**AMBER**
Neydharting Moor-Life Soap/Cleansing Bar	**AUSTRIAN MOOR***
Aloe Vera, Avocado & Cucumber, Green Apple, Jojoba Oil, Just for Men Lather Bar, Orchid Oil, Passionflower, Syndet Beauty Cleansing Bar; *Liquid Soaps:* Aloe Vera, Apricot Kernel Oil, Evening Primrose, French Lavender, Green Apple, Hyacinth, Marigold Flower, Orange Blossom, Passionflower, Tea Rose, Wild Poppy, Woodland Fern	**BARRY M**

BLACKMORES   Marshmallow Soap

BODY & FACE PLACE   Coconut Oil Liquid Soap; *Pure Glycerine Soap:* Green, Lavender, Natural, Rose

BODY CARE*   *Cabashi Range of Liquid Soaps:* Lavender, Ylang Ylang; *Mellow Soap Co. Range of Liquid Soaps:* Almond, Peppermint, Rose Petal, Sandalwood

BODYLINE*   Almond, Coconut Oil, Cucumber & Glycerine, Lavender, Mandarin Orange, Rosewater

BODY REFORM*   *Glycerine Soaps:* Chamomile & Primrose, Comfrey & Marigold, Lavender & Hawthorn, Linden & Elderflower, Orange Flower & Tansy, Rose & Thyme

BODY SHOP   Camellia Oil, Evening Primrose Oil, Jojoba Oil, Tea Rose, Vitamin E, White Musk

BUAV*   Lavender, Orange, Pine, Rats Have Rights

CAMILLA HEPPER*   Avocado Oil, Orange Blossom, Vitamin E

CAURNIE   Almond, Household, Lavender, Mandarin, Original, Rose, Vitamin E

CORNUCOPIA*   *Liquid Soaps:* Lavender, Rosemary

COSMETICS TO GO*   Ben – Son of Miriam, Iso Bar, Juggling Balls, Ko-aloe Bar, Peach Melbar, Rub-a-Dub Scrub, Sand Bar, True Grit

CREIGHTON'S*   Aloe Vera, Apple, Apricot, Avocado, Blackcurrant, Evening Primrose, Fragrance-Free with Vitamin E, Jojoba, Oatmeal, Peach, Strawberry, Tangerine

ENGLISH COUNTRY GARDEN*   *Pure Vegetable Oil Soap:* Lavender, Unperfumed

Lavender, Orange, Pine, Rosemary, Sea-weed

FAITH

Liquid Vegetable Soaps: Damask Rose, English Apple, Lavender & Oatmeal, Vitamin E; *Vegetable Moisturising Soaps:* Coconut, English Apple, Jojoba, Lavender & Oat Meal, Rose Petal

GOODEBODIES*

Natural Organic Soap with Vitamin E, Vitamin E Bar Soap

HOUSE OF MISTRY*

Coconut Oil, Cucumber & Glycerine, English Apple & Vitamin E, Grapefruit & Jojoba

JAMES BODENHAM

Pure Vegetable Oil Soap: Perfumed, Unperfumed

KAYS

Range of soaps

L'AROME*

Chandrika Ayurvedic, Mysore Sandalwood

MANDALA IMPORTS*

Clay, Eucalyptus, Marigold, Menthol, Mint, Rosewater, Sea Moss

MOLTON BROWN*

Blue Orchid Oil Soap; *French Vegetable Soaps:* Cleansing Bars, Green Apple, Lime, Magnolia, Passionfruit, Vanilla; *Vegetable Glycerine Soaps:* Aloe Vera, Cucumber, Jojoba, Peach, Purest Vegetable Cleansing Bar, Vitamin E

MONTAGNE JEUNESSE

Calendula & Evening Primrose Oil, Geranium & Orange, Oatmeal & Aloe Vera, Seaweed, Tea Tree & Lavender

NEAL'S YARD APOTHECARY*

Early Care range: Soap; *Glycerine Soaps:* Aloe, Peach, Vitamin E; *Vegetable Soaps:* Lavender, Orange, Pine, Rosemary

NECTAR

toiletries & cosmetics

PACIFIC ISLE   Jasmine, Plain

PLENTY OF SCENTS   *Pure & Natural Soap (liquid):* Lemon Grass
                       Oil, Unperfumed; *Vegetarian Beauty Soap:*
                       Camomile, Ginseng, Jojoba, Lavender,
                       Lemon

SECRET GARDEN*   *Facial Soaps:* Burdock & Bran, Calendula,
                       Cornsilk; *Natural Glycerine Soaps:*
                       Coconut, Grapefruit, Green Apple, Lemon,
                       Mandarin, Raspberry; *Pure Vegetable
                       Soaps:* Camomile, Elderflower, Lime Flow-
                       er

TIKI   Vitamin E

WELEDA   Iris, Lavender, Rosemary

styling aids

BARRY M   Firm Fix, Soft Set *(hair gels)*

**BODY & FACE
PLACE**   *Hair Gels:* Aloe Vera Ultra, Basic

BODYLINE*   Aloe Vera Hair Gel; *Men's range:* Hair Gel

BODY SHOP   Hair Gel, Slick

CAMILLA HEPPER*   Jojoba Hair Gel

COSMETICS TO GO* Karyan Hair Gel

DANIEL FIELD*   Extra Hold Gel Sap, Fixing Spray, Hair
                       Thickening Lotion, Styling Wax; *(salon use
                       only)* Organic & Mineral Hair Highlighting
                       Treatments, Permanent Organic & Mineral
                       Colour Treatments, Plant Restructurant
                       (reconditioning treatment), Spring Water
                       Perm

GOODEBODIES*   Hair Slick

toiletries & cosmetics

Classic range: Hair Gel	**JAMES BODENHAM**
Seaweed Styling Gel	**MARTHA HILL***
Chamomile Hair Gel	**MONTAGNE JEUNESSE**
Alcohol-Free Styling Gel, Anti-Static Setting Lotion	**SECRET GARDEN***
Solid Brilliantine	**YARDLEY**

sun care

Soothing After-Sun Lotion; *Sun Protection:* Factor 3, Factor 5, Factor 7	**BODY REFORM***
Carrot Sun Range, Cocoa Butter Sun Lotion, Coconut Beach Oil; *Sunscreens:* Maximum Protection, Minimum Protection, Moderate Protection	**BODY SHOP**
Tropical range: After-Sun Soother, Coconut Suntan Oil, Suntan Butter, Suntan Lotion, Suntan Oil	**CAMILLA HEPPER***
After-Sun Dew, Bronzing Lotion, Sun Screen Cream; *Suntan Oils:* Minimum Protection, Moderate Protection	**CARA**
Blocski, Sunproof	**COSMETICS TO GO***
Sun Block: Bronze, Copper; *Sun Cream:* Factor 4–6, Factor 8–10, Factor 15; *Sun Oil:* Factor 2–4; *Sun Vale range:* After-Sun Gelée, After-Sun Lotion	**CREIGHTON'S***
Aloe Gel & Tropical Coconut for After Sun, Bergamot & Sage After-Sun Moisturising Cream	**GOODEBODIES***

toiletries & cosmetics

HONESTY* After-Sun Balm, Tanning Butter; *Sun-Tan Lotions:* High-Protection, Low-Protection, Medium-Protection

JEAN-PIERRE SAND* After-Sun with Liposomes, Pre-Tan Accelerator, Tanning Cream; *Sun Creams:* Factor 4, Factor 8, Factor 15

MARTHA HILL* After-Sun Milk; *Sun Block Cream:* Factor 10; *Sun Block Gel:* Factor 10

MOLTON BROWN* East Wind Island After Sun, Fire Island Sun Oil – Factor 2, Palm Island Sun Lotion – Factor 5, Parasol Hair Protector, Shady Island Sun Block – Factor 8

NEAL'S YARD APOTHECARY* Coconut & Lime Sun Oil, Sesame Sun Oil

NECTAR *Aloe Vera range:* After Sun, Lotion Factor 2, Lotion Factor 4, Lotion Factor 5

PURE PLANT *Multiherb range:* Enriched After-Sun Lotion with Vitamin E, Suntan Lotion with Vitamin E, Suntan Oil with Vitamin E

QUEEN* Suntan Lotion

SECRET GARDEN* After-Sun Soothing Lotion, High-Protection Sun Cream – Factor 10, Medium-Protection Sun Lotion – Factor 6, Sun Bronzer – Factor 2, Suntan Encourager

WINSTONS* Sun Milk

talcum powders

BARRY M Aloe Vera, Apricot Flower, Evening Primrose, Fragrance-Free, French Lavender, Green Apple, Hyacinth, Just for Men Sports, Marigold Flower, Orange Blossom,

toiletries & cosmetics

Tea Rose, Wild Poppy, Woodland Fern

Tea Rose, White Musk; *Mostly Men range:* Talcs **BODY SHOP**

Lavender, Pine, Pure Talc *(hypoallergenic)* **BONITA***

Avocado, Orange Blossom **CAMILLA HEPPER***

Orange Blossom **CHERISH***

Apricot **CREIGHTON'S***

All-Over Body Talc **DAVID HILL***

Old-Fashioned range: Lavender, English Rose, Sandalwood **GOODEBODIES***

Rosewood **GREEN VALLEY**

Baby Powder **JOHNSON'S**

Range of talcs **L'AROME***

Scented Talcum Powder **MARTHA HILL***

Gents, Ladies; *Early Care range:* Talcum **NECTAR**

Epiglow Talc **PURE PLANT**

Coconut, Fresh Green Apple, Grapefruit **SECRET GARDEN***

Talc Powder Puffer **WINSTONS***

Dusting Powders: Black Velvet, Chique, Lace, Pink Lace, White Satin; *Talcs:* Black Label, Black Velvet, Chique, Classic Gold, ESP, Flair, Freesia, Gold, Lace, Lavender, Lily of the Valley, Musk Oil for Men, Musk Oil for Women, Pagan for Women, Pagan Man, Petunia, Pink Lace, Pure Silk, Roses, Sweet Pea, White Satin **YARDLEY**

toiletries & cosmetics

theatrical make-up

LEICHNER
Blending Powder, Cream Cake Make-Up, GP Blood, Greasepaint Form C & G Sticks, Negro Black/Brown, Removing Cream, Spotlight Klear Make-Up

toothpastes

AMBER
Freshmint *(with fluoride)*

AUSTRIAN MOOR*
Neydharting Moor-Life Toothpaste

BLACKMORES
Herbal & Mineral

CAMILLA HEPPER*
Natural Spearmint

CLEAR SPRING
Toothpaste

GOODEBODIES*
Natural Toothpaste

HOLLYTREES*
Fennel, Lemon, Orange

HOUSE OF MISTRY*
Neem Aloe Fennel

INTER-MEDICS
Paradontax Medicinal Toothpaste

KINGFISHER
Fennel, Mint with Lemon *(with fluoride)*

MANDALA IMPORTS*
Vicco Vajradanti Herbal Toothpaste

NELSON'S*
Toothpaste *(unflavoured)*

PIERRE CATTIER*
Dentargile: Aniseed, Lemon, Mint, Rosemary, Sage, Unflavoured

SARAKAN
Toothpaste

WELEDA
Calendula, Herbal, Krameria, Plant Gel, Salt

ZOHAR*
Spearmint Flavour *(with fluoride)*

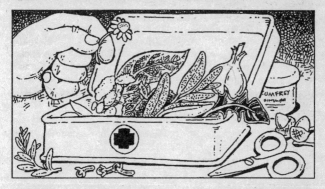

"Prevention is better than cure," runs the old proverb and this holds especially true for those embracing the cruelty-free ethic, for illness and injury can present a dilemma, arising from the fact that all modern prescription drugs are animal-tested. The fact that such 'safe' drugs have been responsible for often serious, and sometimes tragic, side effects in humans is another compelling, if less altruistic argument against their use. In combination with other powerful forces, medical ortho-doxy has created the essentially artificial dilemma of having to choose at times between animal-tested drugs and no drugs at all. It is fortunate therefore that research has indicated that typical vegans and vegetarians are hospitalized considerably less frequently, and for shorter periods, than their omnivore counterparts. In line with this (to *some*) startling finding recent years have seen a substantial increase in the use of vegan and vegetarian diets for therapeutic purposes — including the treat-ment of hypertension, rheumatoid arthritis and certain forms of cancer.

Nevertheless, there are many non-dietary factors at work in determining the state of an individual's health and if we wish to minimize our dependence on a health service that is so heavily reliant on animal experimentation each of us should be prepared to take a good deal more responsibility for our own health than is generally the case. Over and above a healthy diet, a key requirement is a pattern of life that takes due account of the body's need for regular exercise, rest, relaxation, etc. Simple steps like paying close attention to personal and dental hygiene can go a long way to preventing a whole host of minor complaints.

Herbal, homoeopathic and other alternative remedies for common ailments are available at health/wholefood shops, some chemists and by mail order, though many remedies and supplements untainted by animal experimentation nevertheless often contain such ingredients as lactose (milk sugar) as a filler, or are coated in gelatine (from the connective tissue of cattle hides and bones or pigskin), or contain calcium and phosphorous derived from animal bones, or lanolin (from sheep's wool). On the supplementation front it's worth stressing that scientific research has shown that, despite persistent myths to the contrary, even vegans — the most 'extreme' of vegetarians — have no more need than other groups to take vitamin, mineral or any other supplements.

The Vegan Society carries a range of health-related publications — from basic cookbooks to more specialist works on vegan nutrition and veganism in pregnancy and childhood. The latter can prove invaluable in any contacts with health professionals, who are frequently seriously underinformed in matters of nutrition. A full current list can be obtained by writing to: The Vegan Society (Merchandise), 33-35 George Street, Oxford OX1 2AY.

recommended reading

Alternatives to Drugs, Arabella Melville and Colin Johnson, Fontana, 1987

The National Directory of Alternative Aid, (Ed.) Michael E.C Williams, Health Farm Publishing, 1989

Holistic First Aid: A Handbook for the Home, Dr. Michael Nightingale, Optima, 1988

The Vegan Health Plan, Amanda Sweet, Arlington Books, 1987.

Vegan Nutrition: A Survey of Research, Gill Langley MA PhD, Vegan Society, 1988

Full range of homeopathic medicines, including nosodes, allergens and new remedies. Available in various bases to suit requirements *(specify non-lactose)*

AINSWORTH'S*

Wide range of colour therapy products

AURA SOMA*

All 38 flower remedies and the Rescue Remedy *(in liquid form only)*

BACH FLOWER REMEDIES*

Bickiepegs Teething Biscuits

BICKIEPEGS

Aloe Vera Products (Organic): Aloe Vera Food Grade Juice, Aloe Bio *(freeze-dried juice tablet); Ayurvedic Supplements:* Livamine; *Colon Cleansing Programme:* Kali Colonite (Special), Psyllium Husk; *Evening Primrose Product – Premium Grade:* Gamma OL; *Free-Form Amino Acids:* Amino Acid Complex; *Ginseng Products:* Korean Ginseng Extract; *Hair-Care Products:* Bonazi Hair Food Tablet, Bonazi Hair Tonic Lotion, Bonazi Essential Shampoo; *Lecithin Products:* Bioceutics Organic Lecithin *(granules and chewable tablets); Multimineral Supplements:* Bioiodine, Biomagnum, Multiminerals, Super Zinc C; *Slimming Supplements:* Biolina Fresh Water, Psyllium Husk, Slim-Cal 8000; *Vitamin A Supplements:* Biovit A; *Vitamin B Supplements:* Biovit B Complex, Biovite B_6, Biovit B_{12}, Folic Acid, Biovit B_5, Paba; *Vitamin C Supplements:* Biovit C Powder, Bioceutic's Calcium Ascorbate, Bioceutic's Ascrobyl Palmitate, Buffered Vitamin C, Biovit C Tablet, Biovit C Chewable Tablet, Super Biovit C Complex S.R.; *Vitamin E Supplements:* Biovit E Pure Oil; Linseed Oil, Wheatgerm Oil

BIOCEUTICALS

Child-Care Vitamins: Chewable Multivits & Mins, Chewable Vit. C; *General Minerals:* Biocalcium, Biozinc; *Naturetime Sustained-*

BLACKMORES

Release Vitamins: Executive Formula B, B Plus C, B Complex, B_6 – 250mg, Buffered C Complex; Garlix, Bio ACE; *Nutritional Supplements:* PMT Tablets, Brewer's Yeast Tablets, Apple Fibre Chewable Complex; *Specific Herbals:* Agrimony *(diarrhoea)*, Cactus & Hawthorn *(blood pressure)*, Cape Aloes & Cascara *(laxative)*, Celery *(rheumatic)*, Corn Silk *(kidney, bladder)*, Dandelion *(liver)*, Echinesia *(blood)*, Eurphorbia *(asthma)*, Golden Seal *(indigestion)*, Horseradish & Garlic *(catarrh)*, Liquorice *(bronchial)*, Sarsaparilla *(skin)*, Skull Cap & Valerian *(nerves)*, Valerian *(insomnia)*, Witch Hazel *(H.R.)*; *Traditional Herbals:* Alfalfa Tablets, Comfrey, Ginger Tablets, Ginseng Tablets, Horseradish, Kelp, Odourless Garlic, Rosehip Tablets, Raspberry Leaf, Slippery Elm, Watercress & Parsley Tablets; *Vitamins:* ACE, Vitamin A Tablets, Vit. B_1, B_2, B_3, B_5, B_6, Balanced B Tablets, B Complex & Brewer's Yeast, B_{12}, Lemon Bioflav. Complex, Vitamin C 500mg (Protein-Coated), Bio C 1000mg Citrus C with Acerola, Family Multivit & Min, Multivits & Mins

BODY & SOUL* — Skin Clear Cream, Skin Clear Toner *(for problem skins, spots and blemishes)*

BODY MODE* — Winter Blues Inhaler

BODY SHOP — Aloe Heat Lotion *(liniment)*

BOREALIS PRODUCTS* — Insect Repellant

CAMILLA HEPPER* — *Healing Ointments:* Comfrey, Garlic, Leg & Vein, Marigold

CANTASSIUM — *Enzymes:* Bromelain, Co-Q10 Ubiquinone, Lipase – SE Enzyme, Pineapple & Papaya; *Evening Primrose Oil & Polyunsaturates:*

Eve. Primrose Oil Tabs, Eve. Primrose Pure Oil, FFE-200 E.P. Oil & Vitamin E; *Family Vitamins:* Juno Iron, Junokalm, Mini-Junamac 3 Mths–2 Years, Junamac 3–8 Years, Tandem IQ (9–19 Years), Trufree Vits & Mins; Cantamega; *Free Amino Acids & Proteins:* Amino M.S., Aminomega, Antoximega, D.L.P.A. 375, Didamega, Dream-Trim, Foresight Iron, Foresight Minerals, Foresight Vitamins, G.A.B.A., GLO.50 (Glutathione), Histidine, Immuno-mega, L–Carnitine (Pure), L-Cysteine, L-Glutamine, L-Glutamic Acid, L-Glycine, L-Serine, Sportsmega 5000(V), Threonine, Tryptokalm, Tryptophan, Whole Amino Acid Compound; *Ginseng:* FFE Ginseng, Red Pan. Ginseng; *Herbal Remedies:* Alfalfa Fine Ground, Apricot Kernel Nat., Apricot Kernel Powder, Anti-Smoking, Best Agnus Castus, Best Feverfew, Blood Purifying, Bold Herbal Aid for Slimmers, Comfrey, Herb. Aluminium-Free Indigestion, Indigestion (Herbal), Laxative (Herbal), Quiet Days (Prev. Nerve), Quiet Nite Sleep, Quiet Tyme, Rheumatic Pain, Spirulina (Pure), Summer Catarrh, Tong Kwai, Water Loss; *Lecithins:* Lecithin 95 Grans., Lecithin + 5 Combin, Odourless Garlic & Lecithin; *Minerals:* Borodol (Boron & Cal. Combination), B_{13} Calcium, B_{13} Cal. Dri-Fil, B_{13} Chromium, B_{13} Copper, Calcimega, Dolomite, B_{13} Iron, B_{13} Magnesium, B13 Magnesium (Dri-Fil Powder), Mangamac, Organic Germanium, Organic Selenium (Yeast-Free), B_{13} Potassium, Selenium Supplement, Silica Supplement, Super GE-132, Zinc with Mins., Zinc + B_6, B_{13} Zinc, Zinc Lozenges, Zinc + B_6 Drops; *Miscellaneous Health Supplements:* Cantarna RNA, Cantassium Discs, Cardeymin, Cholestastop, Fat Solv. Supplement; No Kola Zip Tabs, Octacosanol, Somanmin, Whole Sel. Alginate; *Multivitamins & Minerals:* Adimac, Canta-mac, Cantavite with FF,

Hair Nutrition Tabs, Vital 4 *(complements Eve. Primrose Oil)*, Womanadds; *Nicotinic Acid:* Nicotinamide, Nicotinic Acid, Sustaniacin; *Slimming Products:* Day-Trim Formula, Glucomannan 500, GP's B-Slim, Night-Trim Formula; *Sun Protection: (Aquamaid label)* Aquatan Tablets; *Vitamin A:* Vitamin A & Beta-Carotene, Vitamin A as Beta Carotene; *Vitamin B:* Vitamins B_1–B_3, B_5, B_6, B_{12}, B_{15}, B_{15} Plus Ginseng; *Vitamin B Complex:* Biotin, Brewer's Yeast *(500mg only)*, Choline, Complete Vitamin B, Full B with Vitamin C, Inositol, P.A.B.A., Whole B Complex; Cantopal; Folic Acid; *Vitamin C & Co-Factors:* Biofla-vonoids, Hesperidin, Quercetin, Rutin, Vitamin C, Vit. C. Natural Powder 75%, Vit. C Pure Powder, Vit. C + E, Whole C. with Bioflavonoids; *Vitamin D:* Vitamin D with Calcium; *Vitamin E:* Vitamin E Tablets; Vit. E Sprout Life, Vit. E – *400 i.u.*; Wheat Germ Oil

COSMETICS TO GO*   Zanzara *(insect repellant)*

DDD LTD   *Spot Removers:* DDD Cream, DDD Medicated Lotion

DOLMA*   Antiseptic & Anti-Viral Body Shampoo, Peppermint & Tea Tree Foot Shampoo *(anti-viral treatment)*

DR VALNET'S*   *Natural Health Care Products:* Alg-Essences *(toner and slimming bath)*, Babibad *(bath for children over 12 months)*, Biobadol *(relaxing and reconditioning bath toner)*, Climarome *(natural decongestant inhalant)*, Dynarome *(soothes tired and swollen legs)*, Flexarome *(muscular fatigue, sensitive joints)*, Tegarome *(antiseptic natural first-aid)*, Volarome *(insect repellant)*

EARTHLORE   B Complex, Calcium + D (EDTA Chelated),

Dolomite + Magnesium/Calcium, Icelandic Kelp, Iron (Gluconate), Magnesium (EDTA Chelated), Mins *(multimineral)* (EDTA Chelated), Potassium (Gluconate), R.N.A. (Yeast-Base Nucleic Acids), Vitamin C (Buffered), Vitamin C (Delayed-Release), Vits *(multivitamin & mineral)*, Zinc (Gluconate)

ERNEST JACKSON

General-Sale Medicines: Antiseptic Throat Pastilles, Bronchial Catarrh Pastilles, Catarrh Pastilles, Cough Pastilles, Envoy Lozenges *(sore throat)*, Nigroids Pellets, Pastilaids *(indigestion)*, Ress Q Pastilles *(mouth ulcers)*; *Pharmacy Medicines:* Night Cough Pastilles, Pholcodine Cough Pastilles

FSC

Minerals: Dolomite (Lead-Free) Tablets, Zinc Lozenges, Zinc Tablets; *Vitamins:* Initial Vitamin Tablets, Vitamin C Tablets Lemon/Lime, Vitamin C Orange Tablets,

HAAR SANA*

Millet Concentrate, Schuppexin Tonic, Super Activator 3 *(hair treatments)*

HEALTHRITE

Multivitamins & Minerals, Ocean Kelp with Added Calcium, Vitamin B Complex, Zinc Gluconate

**HERBAL
LABORATORIES***

Doubleday Comfrey range: Comfrey Oil, Comfrey Tablets; *Herbal Tablet range:* Artiform *(rheumatic pain)*, Backache *(backache)*, Calm Night *(insomnia)*, Catarrh *(catarrh and hayfever)*, Circuform *(circulation)*, Cyst Aid *(cystitis)*, Echinacea *(minor skin conditions)*, Feverfew 125 *(migraine)*, Ladies' Middle of Life *(the menopause)*, Laxative *(occasional constipation)*, Nerve Formula *(tranquillizer)*, Pile *(haemorrhoids)*; *Liquid range:* Barkoff Cough Mixture; *Supplement range:* Barkoff Herbal Lozenges, Oil of Peppermint Tablets

remedies & supplements

THE HERBARIUM*   Comprehensive range of medicinal herbs

HÖFEL'S   Parsley & Garlic Tablets

HOUSE OF MISTRY*   Aloe Vera Juice, Aloe Vera PABA Gel, Calendula Ginseng Aloe Vera PABA Lotion, Calendula Powder; *Creams:* Arnica, Calendula; *Lotions:* Arnica, Calendula

INNOXA*   *41 range:* Spot Treatment Stick

JESSUP MARKETING   Natural Beta-Carotene, Provitamin A

J.L. BRAGG   Medicinal Charcoal Biscuits, Medicinal Charcoal Tablets

LANES   *Remedies:* Charabs Charcoal Tablets, Herbalene, Herbalix, Lusty's Charcoal Tablets, Olbas Oil, Olbas Pastilles; *Tablets:* 1g Vitamin C, B-Plex High-Potency B Complex, Brewer's Yeast, Calcium Supplement, Lusty's Kelp, Spirulina, Top C 200mc, Vitamin B_6 and Herb, Vitamin B_6 High-Potency, Vegevit B_{12}, Zinc; Lecigran, Lusty's Kelp Powder, Wheat Germ Oil Cold-Pressed

LIFEPLAN   Actilife, Boron 3, Brewer's Yeast Special, Buffered C, Calcium Pantothenate, Cal-tabs, Cee Zinc, Chelated Multiminerals, CoQ10, DLPA, Dolomite, Flavorola C Sugarless, Forte-Winx, Hairkare, Happy Garlic, Kelp, Magnezie, Maxifiber, Maximune, SOD 5000, Mineralzinc, Multivits F8 + Iron, Multivits F8 (without Iron), Omnitrace, Quadiron, Quadrazinc, Relaxon, RNA/DNA, Rutin, Selenium Ten, Supazinc, Swiss Hayflower Formula, Thincide 8, Time-Release B Complex, Time-Release C, Vitamin B6, Zinc (Gluconate)

LRC PRODUCTS   *Galloway's* Cough Syrup; *J.E. Ellis*

Buttercup Syrup; *Liquafruta Cough Medicines:* Blackcurrant, Garlic; *Woodward's* Gripe Water; *Wright's* Vaporizer *(for coughs and colds)*

Herbal Tablets, Rasayanas *(herbal food supplements)* — **MAHARISHI AYURVEDA***

Licensed Herbal Medicines: Athera, Bio-balm, Garlodex, Sunerven, Vegetex — **MODERN HEALTH PRODUCTS**

Rollinson's Famous Herbal Remedies: Acne, Anti-Smoking, Catarrh, Constipation, Cystitis, Depression, Hayfever, Heavy Periods, High Blood Pressure, Influenza, Insomnia, Inter-Period Bleeding, Leg Ulcers, Lift Off *(stress relief)*, Lumbago, Period Pains, Piles, Pre-Menstrual Tension, Prostatis, Revive, Rheumatism, Sciatica, Sinusitis, Skin Disorders, Tonic — **NATURAL COUNTRY PRODUCTS***

Herbal Tooth Powder *(for bleeding gums)* — **NATURE'S LTD***

Wide range of natural remedies, incl. medicinal herbs, powders and tinctures — **NEAL'S YARD APOTHECARY***

Enormous range of homeopathic remedies (liquid potencies); Chamomilla Teething Granules, Feverfew Drops, Hypercal *(cuts and sores)*, Pyrethrum *(bites and stings)*; *Homeopathic Creams & Ointments:* Aftersun Cream, Arnica Cream *(bruises)*, Calendula Cream Skin Salve, Contact Dermatitis Cream, Haemorrhoid Cream, Hypercal Cream *(cuts and sores)*, Rheumatic Pain Cream — **NELSON'S***

(herbal food supplement) Oil of Peppermint Fibre Tablets, Oil of Peppermint Powder, Oil of Peppermint Tablets; Japanese Oil of Peppermint *(sprains, stiffness etc.)* — **OBBEKJAERS**

POMPADOUR HERB TEAS	*Medicinal Teas:* Chestea, Digestatea, Nervatea, Sennatea
POTTER'S HERBAL SUPPLIES	*Bottled:* Adiantine, Antispasmodic Drops, Asthma & Chest Mixture, Balm of Gilead, Catarrh Mixture, Comfrey Oil, Composition Essence Peerles, E.P.C. Essence, Herbal Shampoo, Horehound & Aniseed Cough Mixture, Indian Brandee, Indigestion Mixture, Life Drops, Lightning Cough Remedy, Medicated Extract of Rosemary, Nine Rubbing Oils, *Pegina* Indigestion Remedy, Sarsaparilla Liquid, Skin Clear Lotion, Skin Eruptions Mixture, Spanish Tummy Mixture, Stomach Mixture, Tonic & Nervine Essence, Vegetable Cough Remover; *Medicinal Teas:* Kasbah Remedy, Lion Cleansing Herbs; *Tablets:* Acidosis, Anti-Smoking, Chlorophyll, Diuretabs, D1 Stomach, D4 Stomach, Barefoot Feverfew, Garlic, GB *(gall bladder)*, Barefoot Herbprin, Natural Herb *(constipation)*, Neurelax, Passiflora, Rheumatic Pain, Sciargo, Senna, Slippery Elm Stomach, Strength, Tabritis, Tab 337 *(neuritis)*, Tranquilliser; *Ointments:* Corn & Callous, Skin Clear
POWER HEALTH*	Comfrey, Arnica & Witch Hazel Lotion
PURE PLANT PRODUCTS	Aleevex Anti-Chill Bath, Spotoway Cream, Spotoway Tincture
QUEST VITAMINS	Balanced-Ratio Cal-Mag, Enzyme Digest, Multivitamins, Multiminerals, Once a Day Multivitamins & Minerals, Potassium Gluconate, Sitosan, Super Once a Day, Synergistic Magnesium, Synergistic Zinc; *B Vitamins:* Vitamin B_6; *B Complex Vitamins:* Multi B Complex, Mega B Complex, Mega B-50, Mega B-100 Timed Release; *Brite Range (Yeast-Free):* Britekids (Chewable), Briteteens, Britelife; *Hair & Scalp; Jap-*

anese Odourless Garlic (Yeast-Free): Kyolic Super Formula 102, Kyolic Liquid; *Treatment:* Original Bioscalin; *Vitamin C Chewable:* Vit. C 500mg, Vit. C 1000mg; Vitamin E Chewable

Medicinal Charcoal Biscuits **SCOTT'S**

Old Highland Bath Soak; Sea Vegetable Dog Supplement **SEA VEGETABLE CO***

Adexolin Vitamin Drops *("for tiny tots")*, Minadex Tonic *(for babies and children)* **SEVEN SEAS**

Anti-Cellulite Oil, Antiseptic/Acne Lotion, Arthritis Help Oil, Backache Relief Oil, Chilblain Oil, Cold Sore Oil, Eczema/Psoriasis Help Oil, Rheumatic Aches & Pains Help Oil, Sciatica Relief Oil, Sunburn Oil, Varicose Vein Pain Relief **SHANTI***

Amino Acids: L-Arginine Powder, Histidine Complex Tablets, L-Lysine Tablets, L-Ornithine Powder; *Digestive Aids Supplements:* Vegetarian Digestive Aid (Chewable); *Fibre Supplements:* Apple Pectin Powder, Oat Bran Tablets, Psyllium Husks Fibre; *Food Supplements:* Alfalfa Tablets, Brewer's Yeast Powder, Brewer's Yeast Tablets, Vitol – Cold Pressed Wheat Germ Oil; *Lecithin Supplements:* Amplified Granules Vitamin & Mineral Fortified Lecithin Granules, Lecithin '95' Granules, Phosphatidyl Choline 55% Granules; *Mineral Supplements:* Calcium Citrate Tablets, Calcium Magnesium Tablets, Calcium Magnesium Zinc Tablets, Chelated Calcium Tab-lets, Chelated Chromium Tablets, Chelated Copper Tab-lets, Chelated Dolomite Tablets, Chelated Iron Tablets, Chelated Magnesium Tablets, Chelated Manganese Tablets, Chelated Molybdenum Tablets, Chelated Potassium **SOLGAR***

Tablets, Chelated Solamins, Chelated Zinc Tablets, Dolomite Tablets, G.T.F. Chromium Tablets, Kelp Tablets, Magnesium Tablets, Potassium Tablets, Seleno 6 Tablets Yeast-Free Selenium *(50mcg and 200mcg only)*, Zinc 50 Tablets; *Multivitamin & Mineral Supplements:* Formula VM-75 Tablets; *Speciality Supplements:* Antioxodant Factors Tablets, Lipotropic Factors Tablets, Spirulina Powder, Spirulina Tablets; *Vitamin B Supplements:* Biotin Tablets, Folic Acid Tablets, Vitamin B_1 Tablets, Vitamin B_{12} Tablets; *Vitamin B Complex Supplements:* Vitamin B Complex with Vitamin C Tablets; *Vitamin C Supplements:* Calcium Ascorbate Crystals, Calcium Ascorbate Tablets, Citrus Bioflavonoid Complex Tablets, Hy-C Tablets, Rose Hips 300mg Vit. C Tablets (Chewable), Rose Hips Vit. C, Rutin Tablets, Vitamin C Crystals; *Vitamin E Supplements (Natural):* Liquid E, Natural Vitamin E-600 i.u. (Dry) Tablets; *Vitamin K Supplement:* Vitamin K Tablets

TREFRIW WELLS ROMAN SPA LTD

Roman Spa Water *(iron-rich tonic)*

WELEDA*

Arnica Lotion *(muscular pain, stiffness, sprains, bruises)*; Avena Sativa comp. Liquid *(stress relief)*; Birch Elixir *(tonic)*, Blackthorn Elixir *(tonic)*; Calendula Lotion *(healing of cuts, abrasions, minor wounds; mouthwash for sore gums)*; Combudoron Lotion *(minor burns and scalds)*; Copper Ointment *(symptomatic relief of muscular pain)*; Cough Elixir; Feverfew 6X Drops *(anti-inflammatory and for migraine)*; Larch Resin Co. Lotion *(tired and strained eyes)*; Melissa comp. Liquid *(symptoms of stomach ache, occ. diarrhoea, nausea, period pains, toothache)*; Oleum Rhinale. *Homeopathic remedies in (100%-animal-free) liquid form can be obtained from the Weleda dispensary.*

This section covers the myriad items that we use daily in our homes and gardens. Whilst in the case of some commodities — such as adhesives, bedding, upholstery materials and carpetings — the cruelty-free shopper will find life infinitely easier than in the past, with traditionally animal-derived items increasingly giving way to synthetic alternatives, the relative modesty of the range of products listed in the following pages is stark testimony to the commercial sector's continuing overwhelming reliance on animals, especially for testing purposes.

The crude, cruel, and often misleading, animal tests currently employed in the development of mass-market homecare products include:

• *The Draize Eye Irritancy Test*, in which substances are applied to rabbits' eyes over a period of up to seven days with no pain relief. Symptoms may include swelling, haemorrhage, ulceration and discharge;

• *The Draize Skin Test*, in which fur is shaved from the animals' backs and a test substance applied to abraded skin. Symptoms include inflammation, swelling and tissue damage;

• *The LD50 (Lethal Dose 50%) Toxicity Test*, in which a group of animals is dosed (often by inhalation or force-fed by tube) with the test substance to establish the amount which will kill half of them;

• *Teratogenicity Tests*, in which pregnant animals are exposed to the substance by mouth or injection, the young being delivered shortly before term by Caesarian section, studied for abnormalities, killed and sectioned for microscopic investigation. The womb is inspected for young which may have died during the pregnancy.

The cruelty-free shopper can withdraw his/her support for such unethical, and frequently trivial and duplicative, products by simply dispensing with them — especially those labelled as 'new', 'advanced' or similar (i.e. on which *yet more* animal tests have been carried out) — in favour of the cruelty-free alternatives listed in the following pages or elsewhere; and by using 'old-fashioned' basic ingredients, such as salt — for cleaning brass and copper, lemon — for removing stains, and the hundreds of other effective remedies to be found in household encyclopaedias and similar works obtainable in the general reference or household management sections of bookshops. *(See also recommended reading below.)*

The cruelty-free shopper is also alerted to the common use in homecare products of such animal ingredients as lanolin and whey (cleaning solutions); beeswax and shellac (polishes); horsehair, feathers and down (bedding and upholstery); animal wools and silk (yarns and fabrics); and bristles and hair (brushes). Other animal products to steer clear of when buying for the home are materials like bone, horn, ivory, shells, and mother of pearl, which are used for a variety of decorative and ornamental purposes.

If it is true right now that the range of homecare products available to the cruelty-free shopper is still somewhat restricted, readers can be sure that future editions of the *Shopper* will reflect a massive, demand-driven increase, as has been the case with foods, toiletries and cosmetics.

recommended reading

Taking the Pressure Off: What we can do to reduce animal experiments (booklet), RSPCA, 1989
1,000 Handy Household Hints, Lizzie Evans, Octopus, 1989
Conservation at Home: A Practical Handbook, Michael Allaby, Unwin, 1988
Home Ecology, Karen Christensen, Arlington Books, 1989
The Green Consumer Guide, John Elkington and Julia Hales, Gollancz, 1988

air fresheners

Pot Pourri: English Garden, Rose **BODY SHOP**

Pot Pourri: Camilla's Garden, Camilla's Special, Lavender Flowers, Pottergate **CAMILLA HEPPER***

Tudor Rose Pot Pourri **CHERISH***

Odarome *(air purifier)* **DR VALNET'S***

Pot Pourri: Mixed Flower, Purple Haze, Red Rose, Summer Orchard, Verbena Mix **HONESTY***

Sprays: All-Purpose Deodorizer, Perfumed Air Freshener **LITTLE GREEN SHOP***

Boxed Pot Pourri: Citrus, Elizabethan, English Rose, Highland, Nell Gwynn's Recipe; *Manor House Herbarium range:* Office Air Freshener; *Pot Pourri Sachets:* Apple Dash, Citrus, Eastern Promise, Elizabethan, English Rose, Highland, Moorland, Strawberry Fields **POWER HEALTH***

Room Fragrances: 6 varieties **VERDE***

car products

Environment-Friendly range: Self-Polishing Car Wash **GOODEBODIES***

Glass Clean *(spray)*, Panther Polish, Wash & Shine Car Shampoo **LITTLE GREEN SHOP***

cleaning products

Multi-Purpose Household Cleaner, Toilet **ARK**

	Cleaner, Window Cleaner
ATAKA	Ataka bath stain remover and kettle descaler
BIO-D	Multi-Surface Cleaner, Toilet Cleaner
CLEAR SPRING	All-Purpose Cleaner, Cream Cleanser, Liquid Soap, Oven Cleaner, Toilet Cleaner
ECOVER	Alternative Bleach, Cream Cleaner, Floor Soap, Heavy-Duty Hand Cleaner, Toilet Cleaner
GOODEBODIES*	*Environment-Friendly range:* Heavy-Duty Floor Cleanser, Heavy-Duty Hand Cleanser, Kitchen & Bathroom Cleanser, Window Cleaner
GREEN CONNEXION	Three Bio-Grade *(cleans, disinfects and deodorizes)*
HOMECARE PRODUCTS	Bar Keeper's Friend, Copper Glo, Hob Brite, Microwave Plus, Shiny Sinks
HONESTY*	All-Purpose Cleansing Concentrate, Toilet Cleaner
JANCO SALES*	Liquid Concentrate *(multi-purpose liquid soap)*
LITTLE GREEN SHOP*	Barbeque Clean, Descaler HG, Glass Clean *(spray)*, Graffiti Remover, Household All-Purpose Cleaner – Eucalyptus, Green Apple, Wild Flower, Ovenfix Super *(spray)*, Patio Clean, Rapid S *(cream cleaner)*, Roloxid 10 *(algicide)*, Statofix *(carpet shampoo)*, Tantox *(rust treatment)*, Toilex *(toilet cleaner)*
NITOR	All-Purpose Household Cleaner, Glass Cleaner, Toilet Cleaner

homecare products

disinfectants

Disinfectant   **CAURNIE**

Disinfectant   **HONESTY***

Pine Oil Disinfectant   **LITTLE GREEN SHOP***

furniture polish

Furniture Polish   **HONESTY***

Furniture Spray Polish   **LITTLE GREEN SHOP***

gardening products

Q.R. Herbal Compost Maker   **RAYNER & PENNYCOOK***

Marinure range: Extract Liquid Seaweed, Powdered Seaweed Manure   **WILFRID SMITH***

humane mousetrap

Trip-Trap *(mini and maxi).* Catches mice without harming them. Maxi version has space for food and bedding until release.   **WHOLISTIC RESEARCH***

laundry products

ACDO Soap Powder, Glo-White Fabric Whitener   **ACDO**

Laundry Powder, Liquid Detergent   **ARK**

homecare products

BIO-D	Fabric Conditioner, Laundry Liquid, Washing Powder
CLEAR SPRING	Original Laundry Liquid, Washing Powder
ECOVER	Fabric Conditioner, Liquid Clothes Wash, Washing Powder, Wool Wash Liquid
GOODEBODIES*	Fabric Conditioner, Laundry Liquid
HONESTY*	Clothes Washing Liquid
LITTLE GREEN SHOP*	Super Soft *(clothes wash liquid)*

washing-up products

ARK	Washing-Up Liquid
BIO-D	Washing-Up Liquid
CAURNIE	Washing-Up Liquid
CLEAR SPRING	Dishwasher Liquid, Dishwasher Powder, Rinse Aid, Washing-Up Liquid
ECOVER	Automatic Dishwasher Powder, Automatic Dishwasher Rinse Aid
GOODEBODIES*	Washing-Up Liquid
HONESTY*	Dishwasher Liquid, Dishwasher Rinse, Washing-Up Liquid
JANCO SALES*	Liquid Concentrate *(multi-purpose soap)*
LITTLE GREEN SHOP*	Dishwasher Super Rinse, Dishwasher Wash Liquid, Prodish Washing-Up Liquid
NITOR	Washing-Up Liquid
ZOHAR*	Soap Pads, Washing-Up Liquid

The purchase and use of any fur, leather or woollen garment is a consumer vote for misery and death — a disturbing fact, however much obscured by ignorance, inertia and the myth-promoting power of vested interests.

Whether it is made up of farmed or trapped pelts, surely nobody these days can wear a fur coat with an untroubled conscience? "Women who wear furs have a cemetery on their backs," as Brigitte Bardot once put it so graphically. Leather, however, remains widely regarded, not least by 'green' consumers, as a 'legitimate' natural resource. Since the animal has been killed for its flesh why waste the hide, goes one simplistic argument. Few of the many leather-using 'vegetarians' are aware of the extent to which their habit is subsidizing the butchery that they profess to abhor. And as for the general public's view of sheep shearing — well the poor overheated sheep is just having a welcome haircut, isn't it?

So much for the myths, now for the reality.

Unlike leather-yielding farm animals, most *fur-bearing animals* like foxes, mink, ocelots and lynx are reared for their pelts alone. Britain imports around 23 million such pelts a year, with a value of some £200 million. More than 40 million animals worldwide are factory-farmed for the fur trade, and millions of others are caught in steel-jawed traps snapping shut on their legs, or even their snouts and tails. Here in the UK over 50 mink farms produce 250,000 skins annually.

The leather and meat industries are intimately linked, with some 25–50% of slaughterhouse profits coming from sales of the hides of the four million cattle and 15 million pigs slaughtered annually in the UK.

Although wool users are supporting butchery by subsidizing the cost of lamb, mutton and sheep milk, sheep would still be bred and cruelly exploited just for the sake of their coats. Without human interference these animals would grow just enough wool to protect them from the weather, but genetic manipulation has transformed them into wool-bearing monstrosities. Their unnatural overload of wool (up to half their body weight) brings added misery during the summer months when, especially in hot climates, they can die from heat exhaustion. And every year thousands of sheep die of cold soon after the often bloody affair of shearing, generally performed on a piece-work basis. So much for the haircut myth.

Sheep are also routinely subjected to mutilation without anaesthetic. The marking of lambs can involve ear-punching, tail-docking and castration, but perhaps the worst operation, termed 'mulesing', is regularly performed on Merino sheep in Australia, where a combination of heat, wrinkly skin and unnaturally large fleeces makes this breed susceptible to blowfly attack. Wool and skin around the tail are hacked away, leaving a wound which takes weeks to heal. Around 20% of wool in the UK comes from Australia.

The plight of the humble silk worm should not be forgotten in this catalogue of cruel exploitation. Its death is an inevitable part of the production process: when the cocoons are gathered they are all boiled with the worm still inside.

Fortunately, clothes stores and clothing departments of chain stores now carry such a wide range of garments that the choice of quality non-animal clothing is in many cases greater than that of the products of slaughterhouse, farm and trap. Cruelty-free footwear remains a massively underdeveloped area, however. Niche-seeking entrepreneurs take note.

By virtue of rapidly changing fashions the footwear and clothing industries are characterized by a near total lack of product continuity. Even the most up-to-date list of products is therefore of very limited use. As an aid to cruelty-free shopping the following general guidelines are offered, however.

Wool, leather and hide have long since been superseded as the best means of protection against cold and wet conditions. When, for example, did you last see polar expeditions setting off in furs, woolly jumpers and sheepskin-lined boots?!

The cruelty-free shopper in need of *stylish and functional bad weather wear* can choose from a wide range of clothing and footwear made from specially developed fibres and other protective materials. If it's 'breathable' waterproof clothing you want look out for the Gore-tex™ label. For warmth high-quality synthetics — such as those used by Helly Hansen™ and Berghaus™, available from specialists suppliers like Black's of Greenock — will see you through even the most Siberian of winters.

Another specialist supplier is the mail-order firm Cotton On*, which offers a wide range of totally *cotton garments* for both adults and children developed especially with the needs of eczema sufferers in mind. Rainbow Leisure* offers a range of cotton garments, including genuine Guernsey sweaters — an item normally only available in wool. Such suppliers can be a real boon to those who wish to avoid an over-reliance on synthetic fabrics and prefer, for instance, all-cotton nightwear.

For those who feel the need for *look-alike products* (for theatrical use, for example), materials such as the suède-like *Alcantara* and imitation leather fabrics may be obtained from speciality fabric suppliers. Details should be obtainable if you enquire with the fabrics section of any quality department store.

As touched on above, *cruelty-free footwear* remains something of a problem, with the supply of good-quality items both restricted and somewhat erratic. Sturdy and comfortable 100%-non-leather shoes, particularly for men and boys, are hard to come by. Lightweight casual shoes appear in the shops in abundance in the summer months, but perseverance may well be needed in order to find something more formal or serviceable.

In addition to shoe shops proper it's well worth trying sportswear shops (for casuals) and the shoe departments of multiples like British Home Stores, the Co-op, Marks & Spencer and Woolworth. Mail-order and specialist catalogues are also worth scanning. Good-quality shoes made entirely from man-made materials can crop up in unlikely places —

such as among the range of thermal garments sold under the Damart* label.

The ranges of the following leading manufacturers/suppliers of both general and sports footwear have recently been known to include a number of animal-free models: Adidas, Bata, Birkenstock, G.B. Britton (of 'Tuf' fame), Curtess, Derriboots, Diadora, Dunlop, Freeman, Hardy & Willis, Hi-Tec, K Shoes, Lennards, New Balance, Nike, Olivers/Timpson, Olympus, Pirelli, Reebok, Scholl, Stead & Simpson and Tru-Form. Smaller suppliers include Footprints*, importers of Birkenstock shoes from Germany, whose range includes a number of vegan sandals and a clog, and the mail-order firm J.D. Williams & Co. Ltd*, who market a number of non-leather items, including what is described as "an all-weather, wide-fit leisure boot", suitable for men or women. Two more mail-order firms known to have recently carried a number of animal-free footwear lines are Trafford Select* and Burton McCall Ltd*.

For more *specialized needs* it is possible to find bespoke services, such as Marged Shoes*, a cooperative making women's shoes and offering several styles in a tough canvas-type fabric. Staying with out-of-the-ordinary requirements, and showing what is possible with the entrepreneurial will, Diadora do high-quality vegan football boots called 'Loritech', as worn by John Barnes of Liverpool and England. A periodically updated list of 100%-animal-free running shoes is also available from the Vegan Society.

It is not difficult to find stylish *non-leather accessories*, such as bags, purses and wallets, although what is available is frequently dependant on short-lived fashion trends. *(See also* **gift ideas***, for many such items are listed in the merchandise catalogues of pro-animal organizations.)* If something more specialized is required in the way of bags or luggage Camera Care Systems* offer a wide range of ready-made and bespoke merchandise using high-grade synthetic materials.

From mink coats to milk chocolates, and silk dressing-gowns to sheepskin slippers, many of the gifts that help cement human relationships are the last links in a chain of animal exploitation, suffering and premature death. But there is no justification whatever for this state of affairs, for with only a little imagination it is possible to find a wide range of gifts which are cruelty-free and yet are a pleasure to both give and receive.

Look, for example, in the preceding pages under **food products** (confectionery) or **toiletries and cosmetics**. Some firms produce their own attractive gift packs or will make up one of the customer's choosing. You may prefer, however, to bring a more personal touch to bear by making up your very own selection of wholesome goodies. *A hamper of exotica* from the local specialist greengrocer or delicatessen is sure to go down well. *A tasteful selection of vegan wines (see **alcoholic beverages**)* might be just the thing for those who feel the need to raise at least the occasional cup in homage to Bacchus. And few among us, I suspect, would turn our noses up at a gift-wrapped Ogen melon or packet of macadamia nuts.

Kitchenware can make an attractive and well-received gift, especially those items that one would like to have but might hesitate to splash out on for oneself — a juicer perhaps, or an enormous bowl and some wooden platters for all those healthy salads, or maybe a wok for those Chinese stir-frys, or a 'Bel' burger press (cheaply available from almost any department store) for making up large batches of tasty burgers for the freezer. And how about the ultimate designer nutcracker, for those people who like to shell their own? Called the 'Tuffnut', this truly cracking gift is available in quality department stores or direct from the manufacturer, Wakeman Grant*.

When it comes to *paper goods*, look out for the recycled variety, which is now available from many sources in the form of cards, notelets, writing paper and even gift-wrap. Many pro-animal organizations *(see brief list at the end of this section)* offer such items, as well as their own Christmas cards, and sometimes calendars and diaries. Available from one such organization — Animal Aid — is the annual *Living Without Cruelty Diary*, which is a mine of interesting information, facts, figures and addresses. Personal organizers do not have to come bound in leather and an attractive specimen of this much-in-vogue aid to modern life would make an excellent gift. If you have difficulty tracking one down get hold of a catalogue from an ecology-conscious company called The Whole Thing* and you will find a stylish little number bound in black simulated leather, and filled what's more with — yes, recycled paper. This catalogue has lots more to offer — including super juicers, a humane mouse trap and vegan fruit cakes — although it falls somewhat short of cruelty-free: beware of the silk, the royal jelly, the gelatine capsules, etc.

Another catalogue of note comes from Green Farm Nutrition Centre*. It includes such intriguing items as the Calex Wooden Bead Car Seat, which apparently massages your back while you drive; the beechwood Neural Easer, also for massage; and Birkenstock Sport Noppy Sandals, which give your feet a reflexology session while you walk — *ouch!* Or how about 'Sea Bands', which are said to work on acupuncture points and prevent nausea — maybe just the thing for those prone to travel sickness? There are some more conventional items too, like very smart stainless steel pans, water purifiers and attractive pottery burners for aromatic oils.

Lots of good gift ideas can be gleaned from the *merchandise catalogues of charities* working towards an end to many of the injustices in the world. By selecting gifts from their ranges one is, of course, making a further — and, for many, related — ethical statement. OXFAM, for example, states that "through buying crafts and foodstuffs from trading partners committed to economic and social justice, OXFAM aims to help the poor people in developing countries improve their standard of living". Traidcraft is another such organization, committed to supporting small-scale enterprises in the Third World by trading with them. It should be borne in mind, however, that rarely, if ever, are *all* items in such catalogues cruelty-free, for even in relatively enlightened circles low levels of cruelty-consciousness and/or ethical blinkers allow the continuing promotion of animal-based foods and other animal-exploiting goods. Still more regrettably, the same is also true even of the catalogues of major animal welfare (!) charities. Consumer pressure will ultimately remedy this anomaly, particularly offensive in the latter case, so be prepared to do your bit by writing consciousness-raising letters of the "keep up the good work, *but...*" type to offending organizations.

Looking for something *really* different? Well, how about a set of *vegan bagpipes*? Thanks to the march of technology it is now possible to buy bagpipes where the bag is made of the fabric Goretex™ instead of the traditional sheepskin or elk hide. Talking of things Scottish, don't forget you can get a *vegan haggis! (See **food products**, main-courses.)* Returning to things musical, bespoke guitar maker Andy Manson* will make you a *vegan guitar* guaranteed free from the usual trimmings of bone and mother of pearl.

Buying *cruelty-free gifts for children* should not present a problem, but one should try to avoid books and games which reinforce orthodox attitudes and behaviour patterns towards animals — for example, fishing games or Happy Families cards with the smiling butcher and fishmonger. A more progressive Happy Families game, devised by Cath Tate, is available from alternative bookshops and similar outlets, and the Vegan Society publishes a *Children's Books List* giving details of many books that foster a non-speciesist attitude to our fellow creatures. Pets are definitely out as a suitable gift, but how about a 'fluppet' instead? These delightful soft toys which are also hand puppets, come with full instructions on how to look after them and information on the animal itself. The range includes a fox, squirrel, badger and rabbit.

Alternatively, what about *a subscription to a pro-animal magazine*, or *a cruelty-free (i.e. vegan) cookbook*, such as *The Caring Cook: Cruelty-Free Cooking for Beginners*, published by the Vegan Society? More advanced works, including some with a strong gourmet bias, are available from the same source. No list of potential gift books would be complete without Jon Wynne-Tyson's *The Extended Circle: A Dictionary of Humane Thought* and *Food For a Future*. The first is an invaluable anthology and sourcebook, and the second a uniquely powerful presentation of the case for a humane and ecologically sound diet. Both these thought-provoking and inspiring works are available from the Vegan Society.

Animal Aid, 7 Castle Street, Tonbridge, Kent TN9 1BH
British Union for the Abolition of Vivisection, 16a Crane Grove, Islington, London N7 8LB
Dr. Hadwen Trust for Humane Research, 6c Brand Street, Hitchin, Herts SG5 1HX
Hunt Saboteurs Association, PO Box 87, Exeter EX4 3TX
League Against Cruel Sports, 83–87 Union Street, London SE1 1SG
LYNX, PO Box 509, Great Dunmow, Essex CM6 1UH
National Anti-Vivisection Society, 51 Harley Street, London W1N 1DD
Vegan Society, 33–35 George Street, Oxford OX1 2AY
Vegetarian Society, Parkdale, Dunham Road, Altrincham, Cheshire WA14 4QG
Zoocheck, Cherry Tree Cottage, Coldharbour, Dorking, Surrey RH5 6HA

The Cruelty-Free Shopper is compiled on the premise that to be properly described and promoted as 'cruelty-free' a product must be, as far as is possible and practical, entirely free of animal involvement, whether for the purposes of ingredients or testing. To qualify for inclusion in its pages a product must therefore be judged to satisfy two basic criteria: firstly, it must be free of any ingredient of animal origin and, secondly, its production must not involve (non-human) animal testing, where such testing is under the control of the manufacturer.

no animal ingredients

The development and/or manufacture of the product, and where applicable its ingredients, must not involve, or have involved, the use of any animal product, by-product or derivative

Most obviously unacceptable are *items obtained directly from the slaughter of animals* — i.e. meat (incl. poultry and game) and fish *and derivatives thereof* (e.g. meat/fish extracts and stocks).

Other unacceptable items include:

by-products of slaughter — such as bone, hides, skins, hair, bristles, feathers, fur, dried blood, bone-meal, hoof & horn meal, animal fats (e.g. lard, suet, dripping, tallow); gelatine, glycerol, glycerine, stearates (e.g. calcium stearate), stearic acid, fatty acid derivatives, keratin, proteins, amino acids, bone charcoal, pepsin and rennet • *animal-derived additives* — such as 542, 631, 635, 901 *(for further examples see guide to additives and other categories above and below)* • *animal milks* • *animal milk derivatives* — such as lactic acid, lactose, lactates (e.g. sodium lactate) and caseinates (e.g. sodium caseinate) • *dairy products and by-products* — such as butter, cheese, yoghurt and whey • *eggs and their derivatives* — such as lecithin and albumen • *marine animal products* — such as (in addition to true fish) shellfish, whale meat, seal meat, roe, marine oils and extracts (e.g. fish oils, shark oil (squalene), seal oil, whale oil), spermaceti wax, ambergris, isinglass, fish scales • *products from farmed or captured animals* — such as urea, oil of mink, hormones (e.g. oestrogen from urine of pregnant mares) and fixatives (e.g. musk, civet, castoreum) • *bee products* — such as honey, beeswax, propolis, bee pollen and royal jelly • ***animal wools*** • ***natural silk*** • ***miscellaneous other products*** — including lanolin, animal and fish glues, cochineal, carmine, carminic acid, crushed snails or insects, shellac, placenta, amniotic fluids, some vitamins (e.g. D_3)

Where available, vegetable, mineral or plant/mineral-derived synthetic forms of the substances above are acceptable, as are microbiologically-fermented substances of plant origin.

no animal testing

The development and/or manufacture of the product, and where applicable its ingredients, must not involve, or have involved, testing of any sort on (non-human) animals conducted at the initiative of the manufacturer or on its behalf — whether by a parent or sister company, subsidiary, subcontractor, supplier or any other party

Note: It is recognized, however, that few, if any, substances used in commerce will be free of testing on (non-human) animals carried out at one time or another by parties over whom a manufacturer, including a *bona fide* cruelty-free manufacturer, may have no effective control. Both in the UK and abroad, even the most time-proven of purely plant substances have been, and continue to be, animal-tested — frequently to the point (literally) of 'overkill' — in order to forestall lawsuits in litigious markets and/or to satisfy unyielding bureaucratic requirements. Substances so tested include effective alternatives to ethically objectionable animal derivatives. It has therefore been judged expedient to accept for inclusion products involving the use of such substances, *provided that they satisfy the no animal ingredients criterion.*

It is to be hoped that recognition and widespread adoption of the cruelty-free ethic will ultimately compel all companies to abandon (non-human) animal testing in favour of ethical alternatives.

Today, more than ever before, people are aware and concerned about the many thousands of additives which can be found in our food. As a result, public pressure has encouraged supermarket chains to reduce their use in own-brand foods, and since 1986 food labelling laws have enabled concerned shoppers to identify some — although by no means all — of the additives which colour, flavour, emulsify, preserve, thicken, stabilize, glaze, 'improve', bleach, artificially sweeten or regulate the acidity of our food.

In Britain, regulated additives are on a 'permitted list', which covers a number of categories and about 300 substances. There is also a negative or 'black' list of banned additives. Additives approved by the EEC carry 'E' numbers, but there are many used in Britain which are numbered without the 'E' prefix because they have not received EEC approval. Many additives, such as flavourings — of which there are between 3,500 and 6,000 — as well as some enzymes and modified starches, are on neither list because they are not regulated and have no identifying numbers. They are rarely identified individually on food labels; enzymes are not mentioned at all, as they are used as processing aids, rather than being added to the final product, even though contamination may persist.

There are several other aspects of food additives of which the cruelty-free shopper should be aware:

• *animal content* A number of food additives are derivatives of slaughterhouse or other animal substances. Additive number 542 (edible bone phosphate) comes from animal bones, and 631 (sodium 5'-inosinate) from meat waste. Several additives contain stearates, which are sometimes extracted from slaughterhouse fats. Cochineal (E120) is a red colouring which comes from scale insects. Number 920 (L-cysteine hydrochloride) may be obtained from animal hair and chicken feathers. E322 (lecithin) may be either plant-derived (soya beans and other legumes) or animal-derived (eggs) and food labels make no distinction between these two sources.

• *safety and effects on health* Despite or, depending on your viewpoint, to some extent *because of* heavy reliance on (non-human) animal testing *(see below)*, different countries disagree about the safety of various additives. For example, amaranth (E123) is still widely used in Britain (and more than 60 other countries) but has been banned for some years in the

USA, Austria, Finland, Norway and other countries, being suspected of causing cancer. Brown FK (154), another colouring agent, is a potential cancer risk, as are BHA and BHT (E320 and E321) — common antioxidants which are suspected, on the basis of animal tests, of causing birth defects.

A number of additives have been identified by clinical studies as causing allergic and other reactions in sensitive people. Tartrazine (E102) can provoke hyperactivity and migraine in some children, as well as exacerbating asthma, urticaria and eczema. A number of additives, such as brilliant blue FCF (133), sulphur dioxide (E220) and some benzoates (E210–E214) are linked with similar reactions. Other recognized side effects of additives include skin and stomach irritation (e.g. E310–E312), destruction of vitamins and shortness of breath (e.g. E220–E224, E226, E227), and eye and nose irritation and nausea (e.g. E230).

• *animal testing* Many food additives — including some of purely plant derivation — have been tested on laboratory animals such as rats, guinea pigs, rabbits, mice, hamsters, cats and dogs. These testing procedures include a short-term test to determine the single dose of a substance which kills half a group of animals (the LD50 test), causing some animals to suffer loss of appetite, lethargy, diarrhoea, discharge from the eyes and nose, convulsions and nausea. Longer-term tests include 90-day procedures where rats, mice and hamsters receive repeated doses of the additive, and chronic tests which last the lifetime of the animals. Food additives are also given to animals to see if they cause cancer, birth defects or reproductive damage. Many of these tests, involving force-feeding of sometimes toxic substances, cause pain or distress to the thousands of animals used in them each year.

Aside from the purely ethical objections to such experiments, they provide little in the way of clear guidelines on the effect of food additives on people. Animals of different species — and even of the same species but different ages, sex, body weight or strain — vary in their susceptibility to toxic effects. The predicted 'safe levels' of additives may vary as much as 10,000-fold, depending on which statistical method has been used to calculate the extrapolation from animal tests to the human situation. The difficulty is further compounded by the fact that while additives are tested singly in animals over relatively short time periods, some people may consume cocktails of 50–100 additives daily over a period of several decades.

For the reader's convenience two lists are supplied below: the first is of those additives which are known to derive from animals; the second is of additives which *may or may not* be of animal origin, depending on their source or method of manufacture. (All products listed in the *Shopper* containing additives in the second category have been judged, on the basis of information and assurances received, to be animal-free in derivation.)

It is stressed, however, that such lists are of necessity incomplete, since full information is not always available. The use of additive-free products is therefore highly recommended for ethical and health reasons. In response to increased consumer concern on both counts the availability of such products has improved dramatically in recent times, a trend which seems certain to develop further.

animal-derived additives

colouring: E120 • **anti-caking agent:** 542 • **flavour enhancers:** 631, 635 • **glazing agents:** 901, 904 • **improver:** 920 • **unnumbered:** calcium mesoinositol hexaphosphate, spermaceti, sperm oil, lactose

possibly animal-derived additives

any unspecified 'flavourings' • **colourings:** E101, E101a, E153 • **preservatives:** E203, E213, E227, E252, E270, E282 • **emulsifiers, thickeners, stabilizers, antioxidants:** E302, E322, E325–E327, E333, E341a–c, E404, 430-436, E470, E471, E472a–e, E473–E475, 476, E477, 478, E481–E483, 491–495 • **solvent, sweetener:** E422 • **anti-caking agents:** 570, 572 • **flavour enhancer:** 627 • **unnumbered:** butyl stearate, calcium heptonate, calcium phytate, glyceryl diacetate, diacetin, glyceryl monoacetate, monoacetin, glyceryl triacetate, triacetin, glycine, leucine, oxystearin

There are several useful books which explore the issue of food additives in some depth. These include *The New E for Additives*, by Maurice Hanssen and Jill Marsden (Thorsons, 1987), and *Additives — Your Complete Survival Guide*, by Felicity Lawrence (Century, 1986), both of which contain detailed individual descriptions of the source, function and possible toxicity of all known additives. *Food Additives — Taking the Lid off What We Really Eat*, by Erik Millstone (Penguin, 1986), and *Understanding Additives* (The Consumers' Association and Hodder and Stoughton, 1988) explain arguments for and against the use of additives, and their possible effects on health. All four books contain criticisms of animal safety testing and call for better labelling.

Aethera, 4 Felindre, Lon Hendre, Waun Fawr, Aberystwyth SY23 3PY • **Ainsworth's**, 38 New Cavendish St, London W1M 7LH • **Andy Manson**, Wyndham House, Bondleigh, North Tawton EX20 2AN • **Aura Soma**, DEV Aura, Little London, Tetford LN9 6QL • **Austrian Moor**, White Ladies, Maresfield TN22 2HH • **Bach Flower Remedies**, Mt Vernon, Sotwell, Wallingford OX10 0PZ • **Back To Nature**, PO Box 38, Flitwick MK45 5NT • **Beauty Without Cruelty**, 37 Avebury Ave, Tonbridge TN9 1TL • **Body & Soul**, Sarnett House, Repton Dr, Gidea Park RM2 5LP • **Bodyline**, Unit 4/5, Alders Way, Yalberton Ind Est, Paignton TQ4 7QL • **Body Mode**, Unit 14, 5a Wyvern Way, Uxbridge UB8 2XN • **Body Reform**, Unit 5, Kingsway Buildings, Bridgend Ind Est, Mid Glamorgan CF31 3SD • **Bonita**, 23 Archer's Close, Droitwich WR9 9LH • **Borealis**, Old Pier Rd, Broadford, Isle of Skye • **BUAV**, 16a Crane Grove, London N7 8LB • **Burton McCall**, Samuel St, Leicester LE1 1RU • **Camera Care Systems**, Vale Lane, Bedminster, Bristol BS3 5RU • **Camilla Hepper**, 18/19 Mountbatten Rd, Kennedy Way, Tiverton EX16 6SW • **Chandoré**, 2 Ashtree Ave, Mitcham CR4 9AR • **Charles Perry**, English Estates Building, Carminnow Rd, Bodmin PL31 1EP • **Cherish**, 34 Woodlands Ave, West Byfleet KT14 6AT • **Cornucopia**, 50 The Half Croft, Syston, Leicester LE7 8LD • **Cosmetics to Go**, 29 High St, Poole BH15 1AB • **Cotton On**, 29 Clifton St, Lytham FY8 5HW • **Crane Sea Vegetables**, Mill Farm Cottage, New Aberdour, Fraserburgh AB4 4HR • **Crescent**, Tyler Hill, Canterbury CT2 9NG • **Crimpers**, 63–67 Heath St, London NW3 6UG • **Damart**, Bingley BD97 1AD • **Daniel Field**, 23 Topsfield Parade, London N8 8PP • **David Hill** – as for **Martha Hill** • **Diana B** – as for **Little Green Shop** • **Dolma**, 19 Royce Ave, Nottingham NG15 6FU • **Dorchester Chocolates**, Poundbury West Ind Est, Dorchester, Dorset • **Dr Valnet**, PO Box 407, Addlestone, Weybridge KT15 3TE • **Eliko**, Unit 1, 12/48 Northumberland Pk, London N17 0TX • **English Country Garden**, 17 Hanover Place, Worcester Rd, Bromsgrove B61 7DT • **English Lakes**, Freepost, Kendal LA8 8BR • **Enolacto**, 3 Belsize Mews, London NW3 5AT • **Fleur**, 8 Baden Rd, London N8 7RJ • **Food Watch**, Butts Pond Ind Est, Sturminster Newton DT10 1AZ • **Footprints**, Oak Tree Barn, Lower Velwell, Dartington TQ9 6AD • **Frangipani**, 28 The Arcade, Broadmead, Bristol BS1 3JD • **Garland**, Borrowdale, Storeton Lane, Barnston L61 1BU • **Glenny Brewery**, Station Lane, Witney OX8 6BH • **Goodebodies**, 20 Victoria Ave, Harrogate HG1 5QY • **Green Farm Nutrition Centre**, Burwash TN19 7LA • **Haar Sana**, PO Box 1717, London W9 1DQ • **Happidog Petfoods**, Bridgend, Brownhill Lane, Preston PR4 4SJ • **Herbal Laboratories**, 44 Victoria Rd West, Cleveleys FY5 1BU • **The Herbarium**, 11 Oxford Rd, Altrincham WA14 2DY • **Highland Wineries**, Moniack Castle, Kirkhill, Inverness • **Hollytrees**, 26 Hudson Rd,

mail-order addresses

Bexleyheath DA7 4PQ • **Honesty**, 33 Markham Rd, Chesterfield S40
1TA • **House of Mistry**, 15–17 South End Rd, London NW3 2PT •
Janco Sales, 11 Seymour Rd, Hampton Hill TW12 1DD • **Jean-Pierre
Sand**, Ramsgate Rd, Sandwich CT13 9QS • **Kittywake**, Llandeilo
SA19 7DP • **L'Arome**, Parkway, Deeside Ind Pk, Deeside CH5 2NS •
Little Green Shop, 8 St George's Place, Brighton BN1 4GB •
MacSweens, 130 Bruntsfield Place, Edinburgh EH10 4ES •
Maharishi Ayurveda, Mentmore Towers, Leyton Buzzard LU7 0QH •
Mandala Imports, 7 Maple Rd, Horfield, Bristol BS7 8RD • **Marged
Shoes**, Stable Cottage, Derry Ormand Park, Betys Bledrws, Lampeter
SA48 8DA • **Mark Richardson Trading**, 290 Fulham Palace Rd,
London SW6 6HP • **Martha Hill**, Freepost, Corby NN17 3BR • **Meg
Rivers** – as for **The Whole Thing** • **Molton Brown**, Motts Hall,
Gaunt's End, Elsenham, Bishop's Stortford CM22 6DR • **Murphy &
Son**, Alpine St, Old Basford, Nottingham NG6 0HQ • **Natural Country
Products**, as for **Back to Nature** • **Nature's Ltd**, 212 Watford Way,
London NW4 4UA • **Neal's Yard Apothecary**, 2 Neal's Yard, London
WC2 • **Nelson's**, 5 Endeavour Way, London SW19 9UH • **Oxfam
Trading**, Murdock Rd, Bicester OX6 7RF • **Pecksniff's**, 45–46
Meeting House Lane, Brighton • **Pierre Cattier**, Island Farm Ave,
Molesey Trad Est, East Molesey KT8 0UZ • **Power Health**, 10 Central
Ave, Airfield Est, Pocklington YO4 2NR • **Queen**, 130 Wigmore St,
London WH1 0AT • **Rainbow Leisure**, 92a Elm Grove, Hayling Island
PO11 9EH • **Rayner & Pennycook**, PO Box 146, Weybridge KT13
0SQ • **Romany** – as for **Power Health** • **Sea Vegetable Co**, Pitkerrie,
Balmuchy Fearn IV20 1TN • **Secret Garden**, 153 Regents St, London
W1R 8HQ • **Shanti**, 148 London Rd, Temple Ewell CT16 3DE •
Solgar, 260–300 Berkhamsted Rd, Chesham HP5 3EZ • **Stargazer**,
PO Box 609, London SW3 4NS • **Traidcraft**, Kingsway, Gateshead
NE11 0NE • **Trafford Select**, London Rd, Preston PR1 4DD • **Verde**,
4a, 11 Long St, London E2 8HJ • **Vinature**, 16 Cotton Lane,
Birmingham B13 9SA • **Vinceremos**, Beechwood Centre, Elmete
Lane, Leeds LS8 2LQ • **Vintage Roots**, 25 Manchester Rd, Reading
RG1 3QE • **Wafcol**, The Nutrition Bakery, Haigh Ave, Stockport SK4
1NU • **Wakeman Grant**, 3 Longs Lane, Stubbington PO14 2ET • **The
Watermill**, Little Salkeld, Penrith CA10 1NN • **Weleda**, Heanor Rd,
Ilkeston DE7 8DR • **The Whole Thing**, PO Box 100, Altrincham WA14
5SZ • **Wholistic Research**, Bright Haven, Robin's Lane, Lolworth
CB3 8HH • **Wilfrid Smith**, Gemini House, High St, Edgeware,
Middlesex • **J.D. Williams & Co**, Dale St, Manchester • **Winston's**,
York House, York St, Bradford BD8 0HR • **Zohar**, 73 Windsor Rd,
Prestwich M25 8DB

index

index

notes